HELP FOR THE HANDICAPPED CHILD

Other books by Florence Weiner:

HOW TO SURVIVE IN NEW YORK
WITH CHILDREN (1969)

AROUND WESTCHESTER WITH
CHILDREN (1970)

PEACE IS YOU AND ME (1972)

HELP FOR THE HANDICAPPED CHILD

by Florence Weiner

McGraw-Hill Book Company
New York St. Louis San Francisco Düsseldorf
London Mexico Panama Sydney Toronto

First Edition

123456789BPBP79876543

Library of Congress Cataloging in Publication Data

Weiner, Florence.
  Help for the handicapped child.

  1. Handicapped children—Rehabilitation. I. Title.
[DNLM: 1. Child health services—U.S.—Directories.
2. Handicapped. 3. Rehabilitation—Directories.
HD 7256.U5 W423h 1972]
RJ138.W45 1973   362.7′8′40973   72-7451
ISBN 0-07-069048-0

This book is for Dr. Edith Schröder
and her colleagues in the helping professions.

Preface

Someone once asked Abraham Lincoln, "What do you do when you come to the end of your rope?" He answered, "Tie a knot in it and hang on." Parents of a child with a handicap silently ask this question many times. They often feel that no one cares; that they, who need the most consideration, seem to receive the least.

Parents suffer guilt, anxiety, frustration, tension, anger, weariness, impatience—and the overwhelming problem of finding someone to whom they can turn to help share the burden. The problems of a child with a handicap, then, become the concern of each member of his family. How they cope with these problems affects each of them.

When parents attempt to find help in their community, they often become discouraged by the lack of services and the impersonal attitude of administrators. In the end, they may turn away from whatever assistance is available. There are, however, people in private and public agencies whose work it is to fulfill the medical, educational, and recreational needs of handicapped children. It seems important to describe these sources of help throughout the United States both for the family financially and emotionally overwhelmed with their problem and for the family that can afford private medical care but often overlooks available services. It is hoped that this book will also be helpful to physicians, teachers, social workers, ministers, and others who make referrals.

Community resources, such as visiting nurse services, homemaker-home health aide services, speech therapists, outpatient services of medical and dental schools, and university health services are described in this book.

State health services vary from state to state. However, in each state the Crippled Children's Program generally offers free or low-cost diagnostic services to all, regardless of economic status, based on the assumption that a diagnosis is usually necessary to estimate the overall cost and duration of treatment. The state agencies administering health services are listed both for those financially eligible and for families who might otherwise be able to afford private medical care but wish to consult specialists in these clinics.

Voluntary health associations—United Cerebral Palsy, Muscular Dystrophy, and the Easter Seal Society, for example—maintain clinics with a wide range of services such as speech therapy, physical therapy, and recreational activities; arrange for transportation in some places; and sponsor special education programs. They also offer the opportunity for families with similar problems to come together, offer strength and comfort, share experiences and information. The services of both the national headquarters and local affiliates of the association for each handicap are described.

The National Institutes of Health (NIH), an agency of the Department of Health, Education, and Welfare, serves as administrator of federal funds which help support reasearch by scientists in universities, medical schools, hospitals, clinics, and other nonprofit research and teaching institutions. Although the Institutes are not directly involved in health services, they maintain hundreds of laboratories where research into many of the handicaps of children are conducted. Some recent research at each Institute is outlined.

In addition to the services for children with a particular handicap, a nontechnical description of the condition is often needed, as well as a discussion of which professional category is concerned with their special problem; what treatment is necessary; and which tests have to be given. It is helpful to know the most recent medical progress that may benefit a child and the meaning of the technical words used by the physician. These needs are covered in each category.

America, one of the wealthiest nations, is not necessarily the healthiest. Although medical research has yielded important advances they are not available to all who desperately need them. It is not unusual for a child with hemophilia to require prophylaxis, the constant replacement of blood to combat bleeding episodes, costing $12,000 to $22,000 a year. Three dialysis treatments a week on an artificial kidney machine in a profit-making hospital or kidney center costs up to $36,000 a year. For thousands of children this help is out of reach.

And yet great changes are taking place in this country. More effort is being placed on achieving increased health services for everyone. In our lifetime we have seen the development of a vaccine for polio and rubella, antibiotics, open-heart surgery, and anticoagulants. It is possible to hope that tomorrow researchers will make discoveries that will help many thousands of handicapped children. For their parents hope is the secret weapon.

FLORENCE WEINER

Acknowledgments

I would like to express my appreciation to the medical committees and staff of the voluntary health associations, who were enormously helpful. Dr. Frances A. Reeder, Assistant Director, Bureau of Medical Rehabilitation, New York State; and Dr. Beatrice Slater, Bureau of Handicapped Children, New York City, made many helpful suggestions particularly from the aspect of state and city health services. Guy M. Moore of the Office of Information, the National Institutes of Health, Bethesda, Maryland, made available information of current research at the Institutes benefiting handicapped children.

I am indebted to the medical consultant of the book, Dr. Peggy Alsup, Supervising Physician, Sickle Cell Clinic of Syndenham and Knickerbocker Hospitals, and a practicing physician who brought her wide experience in treating handicapped children, and a special gentleness that I shall not soon forget.

Contents

xiii INTRODUCTION

by Charles A. Janeway, M.D.

Part One
HANDICAPS

  3 Allergies/Asthma
 14 Arthritis and Related Rheumatic Diseases
 21 Birth Defects
 30 Blindness and Partial Sightedness
 42 Cancer/Leukemia
 53 Cerebral Palsy
 59 Cooley's Anemia
 63 Cystic Fibrosis
 70 Deafness/Partial Hearing
 78 Dental Problems
 83 Diabetes
 89 Drug Addiction
 93 Epilepsy
102 Heart Disease
111 Hemophilia
117 Kidney Disease
     Learning Disabilities/Minimal Brain
124   Dysfunction
130 Mental Illness/Autism
147 Muscular Dystrophy
     Orthopedic and Physically Handicapping
155   Conditions
156 Retardation
165 Sickle-Cell Anemia
169 Tay-Sachs Disease
172 Tuberculosis
177 Venereal Disease

Part Two
181 **GENERAL INFORMATION**

183 COMMUNITY SERVICES
183 Local Departments of Health
184 Community Councils Information Services
184 Religion-Affiliated Services
185 Homemaker-Home Health Aides
185 Visiting Nurse Services
186 Speech Therapists
186 Physical Therapists
187 Services of Medical and Dental Schools/
  University Services
187 Fraternal Health Services

  STATE SERVICES FOR HANDICAPPED
189 CHILDREN
189 Description of Crippled Children's Program
  State Agencies Administering Services for
192   Handicapped Children
196 Special Education
196 Rehabilitation Services

198 GOVERNMENT SERVICES
198 National Institutes of Health
205 Library Services
206 Tax Deductions

  HEALTH PLANS AND INSURANCE
207 INFORMATION
207 Group Health Insurance Plans
208 Insurance Information

209 RECREATION FOR THE HANDICAPPED
209 Scouts
209 Summer Camps
210 Recreational Programs

211 EMERGENCY SERVICES

213 **INDEX**

Introduction

This book should fill a real need for parents who suddenly find themselves faced by a new problem —the presence in their family of a handicapped child. Whether this problem has arisen as a result of inheritance, of unknown events during pregnancy, or of disease acquired after birth, it is never expected. Most of us are optimists at heart, and parents, except in families with known hereditary diseases, assume that their newborn baby will be normal, as he or she will be, in the vast majority of cases. Once a handicap or potential handicap has been identified, the parents must deal with several major issues—first, how to face their own sense of guilt, anger, and depression so as to be as competent and loving parents as possible; second, how to assure that the handicapped child gets the best possible medical and social care available without "spoiling" him or "driving" him too hard; and third, how to deal with this new child in such a way that his brothers and sisters who are normal will neither resent him nor feel neglected themselves.

In primitive societies, a handicapped child rarely survives infancy, and may even be left exposed to die. In the desperately overcrowded and poverty-ridden villages and city slums of many Asian countries, handicapped children are often hidden in the back of the house and have little future but to become beggars. In Western society, our first response to this problem— particularly in the case of mental retardation or neurological impairment—was the institutionalization of such children, often as early as possible. Modern studies in psychology and child development have shown that institutionalization itself, particularly in infancy, may have a handicapping effect on mental and social development.

Today, therefore, the emphasis, more and more, is on providing special facilities for the treatment or education of handicapped children in their own communities, so that they may remain at home, at least in their early years, whenever this is possible.

A typical American response to a handicapped child is, "Let's do something about it." The voluntary health association, usually formed by parents of such children, often assisted by concerned professionals and a few public-spirited citizens with organizing ability, is a peculiarly American institution; it is set up to work for better care for the victims of handicapping disease, to channel the generosity of the public, and to influence legislators to appropriate governmental funds for the improvement of facilities, development of better treatment programs, and support of research on the cause, prevention, and amelioration of the disease. These associations, starting with the National Association for Mental Health and the National Foundation for Infantile Paralysis, have been the prototypes of a host of organizations, large and small, which *in toto* have had a significant impact on medical and social care, medical research, and public policy in this country.

This book providés a valuable introduction to the labyrinth of services—both public and private—to which the parents of handicapped children can turn for help in this country. By bringing all the information on governmental services, privately supported services, and voluntary health agencies together in one informational guide, both the parents and their professional advisers—physician or social worker—have a ready reference to the major resources to which they can then turn for assistance. To my knowledge this type of information, for the majority of handicaps which affect children, has not been brought together in one ready reference book before. It therefore should be made available in the office of every physician caring for children and of all those public and private agencies which provide help to families in difficulty.

CHARLES A. JANEWAY, M.D.
Physician-in-Chief,
Children's Hospital Medical Center
Boston, Massachusetts
December 8, 1972

Part One
HANDICAPS

Allergies/Asthma

ALLERGIES

DESCRIPTION OF
CONDITION

An estimated thirty-one million Americans suffer from some type of allergic disease, ranging from mild hay fever to severe, crippling asthma. Asthma and hay fever rank third in prevalence among all chronic disease, and first among children's diseases.

Allergy is a form of harmful sensitivity developed in living tissues of the body by exposure to substances ordinarily harmless. When invaded by threatening foreign matter, such as bacteria and viruses, the body produces *antibodies* to defend itself. The allergic person's body mistakenly produces antibodies against harmless things like pollen grains. In the case of hay fever, for example, when pollen grains are breathed in, antibodies produced by the allergic person combine with them and stimulate white blood cells to release an irritating chemical called *histamine*. Histamine causes the unpleasant symptoms associated with hay fever.

Hundreds of substances produce allergy. The air-borne causes include pollens of plants, spores of many fungi or molds in farms and homes, house dust, animal dander, feathers, mattress and furniture stuffing, ingredients of cosmetics, metals, and dyes. Foods such as nuts, chocolate, fruits, cereal, and shellfish may be responsible for persistent symptoms. Particularly in infants and very young children, milk, eggs, and oranges may be irritants.

Two relatively different types of allergy have been identified in human beings. One can be acquired by almost anyone who is exposed to certain substances. Typical examples of this type are contact eczema produced by poison ivy and serum sickness, which occurs about a week after injection of horse serum, given as antitoxin to prevent lockjaw. The second type seems to arise from some inherited predisposition. This has been called *atopy* and is represented by hay fever, asthma, and infantile eczema.

Many drugs and chemicals are responsible for allergic reactions, especially frequently used aspirin, sulfa drugs, and penicillin.

Allergy has recently been implicated in a great many diseases of the blood vessels, nervous system, joints, kidneys, digestive tract, eyes, and ears. The course and form of many recognized infectious diseases, such as tuberculosis and rheumatic fever, can best be explained on the basis of allergic response.

TREATMENT   In treating the patient with an allergy, a thorough record of the patient's history, a physical examination, and laboratory testing are essential. This background information is needed to determine the presence of the allergy and detect its cause.

Once the cause of an allergy is determined, the most successful principle in treatment is to remove it and thus eliminate the symptoms.

In the case of offending foods, absolute or partial restriction of these from the diet will be determined by the individual's progress and continued evaluation by the physician.

If an air-borne cause is difficult to avoid, such as dust, molds, and pollen, immunization by injection may be recommended to build up a lasting immunity or resistance. The process is called desensitization and is done by injection of small but increasing amounts of solutions of the harmful substance.

A type of substance recently tested, but not in wide use, may prove with continued research to be highly effective in alleviating and perhaps preventing the symptoms of allergies. The substance, called an *allergoid*, works on the same principle as the toxoid used to vaccinate people against diphtheria. It produces allergy, but has been sufficiently "detoxified" so that it can stimulate resistance without causing serious allergy symptoms. Ragweed pollen, for example, might be used as an allergoid in the treatment of hay fever.

Researchers have found that allergic persons produce antibodies as a defense in response to pollen. These, however, cannot function effectively because another antibody, which prevents the release of histamine, is also present. A treatment of sensitizing injections thus builds up the allergic person's reserves of "blocking" antibodies without producing enough histamine to cause unpleasant symptoms.

In current practice, *hyposensitizing* injections consist of small doses of the *allergen* or an extract of it. The effectiveness of the injections is limited because, if too much allergen is given, it will cause allergy symptoms. By using the allergoid, considerably higher doses of allergen may be used and may thus build up much higher levels of "blocking" antibodies without causing allergic symptoms.

NOTE: Allergic children should receive the same immunizations as nonallergic children against diphtheria, tetanus, smallpox, whooping cough, measles, and polio. The injections are usually well-tolerated. When a reaction is feared due to extreme sensitivity, a fraction of the dosage may be injected and the rest of the vaccine given in several later doses.

PROGNOSIS Early recognition and treatment of allergic diseases is most important. One of the chief characteristics of most allergies is that, although they can be cured early in their course, they can lead to serious irreversible complications if neglected.

MEDICAL PROGRESS The application of what is already known about allergy can help the majority of allergic children and cure many of them. Continued progress has been made in describing the nature of "allergic" antibodies accompanied by studies of the allergens, which are the proximate cause of the disease.

FUTURE MEDICAL GOALS

There are many important unanswered questions about allergic diseases. Some of them are:

What happens when the sensitized antibody links up with its target allergen?

What products are released and what are their specific reactions in the body?

Why are some parts of the human system sensitive to a specific allergic reaction, while others are not?

What, specifically, is the genetic factor that links the allergy of a son to the predisposed but different allergy of his father or his grandfather?

Although there is hope that these questions can be answered through research, there are also some disturbing signs that environmental conditions are growing worse for the individual with respiratory ills, allergic and otherwise. No city seems to be immune to air pollution. Experts from coast to coast have warned that many cities are on the brink of the kind of disaster that hit London twice in recent years, claiming nearly 4,400 lives. New and more effective methods must be found to clean the air.

DRUG THERAPY

See page 4 for a description of desensitization injections.

Although in a small percentage of patients, for reasons not yet clear, hyposensitization fails to control allergic diseases, this method of immunotherapy still offers the best opportunity for a consistent safe control of allergic rhinitis and allergic asthma in cases where avoidance of exposure to the allergen is impossible.

Treatment with drugs to control symptoms also is an important adjunct in management of allergic diseases. During the last decade, a group of drugs, known as antihistamines, have proven valuable particularly for treating hay fever and hives and controlling itching.

The beneficial effects of such hormones as ACTH, cortisone, and synthetic cortisonelike drugs have been a tremendous boon in certain types of allergy. These drugs produce profound changes and many patients cannot tolerate them.

They are administered with caution and under close medical supervision.

TESTS

Scratch Tests—The patient's history, symptoms and examination usually give enough evidence for the diagnosis of the allergic ailment, but scratch tests are given to make the diagnosis more accurate to help narrow down the field of suspected causes of the patient's allergy.

They are administered by placing powdered or liquid allergens on scratches, or injecting their solutions into the skin. A positive result is shown by an itching bump that looks like a mosquito bite which appears within a few minutes. (Air-borne allergens—for example, dust, pollens, and molds —yield more reliable results than food allergies.) To further pinpoint the cause of an allergy, foods or inhalants may be removed and the reaction studied.

Intradermal Tests—These tests are administered by placing a minute amount of the extract into the layers of the skin. These are observed after about fifteen minutes. A positive reaction indicating sensitivity appears as a red, itching, elevated area closely resembling a hive or insect bite. A negative test does not preclude the presence of an allergy nor do multiple positive reactions necessarily mean each positive substance is present. Every positive reaction must be correlated with symptoms and history.

Passive Transfer Testing—In some very young children, where skin testing is impractical, a sample of the child's blood serum can be injected into the skin of a non-allergic person, who then receives the skin test. Known as "passive transfer testing," this method is also used where the patient's skin is extremely sensitive or where there is an extensive rash.

Patch Tests—To determine the allergen in contact dermatitis, a patch test rather than a scratch test is preferable to isolate the irritant. The material, or an extract of it, is placed on the skin, covered with a patch, and the area is examined for a reaction a day or two later.

ASTHMA

DESCRIPTION OF
CONDITION

Asthma attacks appear as a shortness of breath with coughing and wheezing, and a choking feeling caused by obstruction of the small bronchial tubes, either by the swelling of the membrane lining or the tubes; or by contraction of the muscles around the tubes; or by plugging of the tubes by mucus. As a result, the lungs become distended because all of the air cannot be exhaled— although air *can* be breathed in. The chest swells, there are wheezing noises, the neck muscles strain, the veins become engorged, and the sufferer, as a result, often cannot lie down. The suffering is severe, may last for a few moments, hours, or days at a time.

Although the patient may be in intense distress, the condition is rarely fatal when good medical care is obtained. The complications of asthma, however, may be far-reaching. The most serious and frequent complication is the permanent stretching of the lung sacs so that they become permanently distended, losing the capacity to expand and contract with the bellowslike motion of normal efficient breathing.

There are various causes of asthma, such as a reaction to bacterial or virus infections, principally those involving the sinuses, throat, and bronchi. In other cases, the patient seems to react to bacteria in his own body just as he might react to an allergen from any other source. In either case the infection is the cause of the asthma.

By far the most common type of asthma is that produced by allergens. This is a condition of sensitivity which certain persons may develop to substances ordinarily harmless. These sensitizing substances may be taken into the body by inhaling air, by being swallowed, by contact with the skin, or by being injected. Emotional excitement, laughter, overexertion, or even ordinary activity may act as a "trigger."

Asthma presents special psychological problems, since attacks are often unexpected and frightening, not only to the child but to those around him. Time lost from school and limitations in his activities tend to make a child feel different. He may become overdependent and preoccupied with his illness, perhaps hostile and aggressive, and generally more easily distressed. These emotional problems may, in turn, aggravate the condition.

TREATMENT The severity of asthmatic attacks varies from patient to patient and from time to time in the same patient. It can be mild and uncomplicated and appear only occasionally. In mild cases the symptoms may be barely noticeable at rest, but may be quite apparent after exertion.

The medical needs of the asthmatic are as follows: immediate relief from the acute attack and reduction of chronic symptoms, such as shortness of breath, wheezing, and coughing. Treatment is directed toward control of acute attacks, minimizing the frequency of attacks, and reducing symptoms.

For easy breathing the bronchial tree must be kept clean so that the airways remain open. Under a physician's supervision, breathing exercises and a proper physical fitness regime may be instituted in addition to medication.

PROGNOSIS The outlook is good, but it depends on how early diagnosis, care, and treatment are instituted. In the majority of cases children's asthma can be controlled and relieved with proper modern care by a specialist and the cooperation of parents, siblings, and the patient. Many cases that were considered hopeless a few years ago can now be helped. The child does not "outgrow" asthma, however. The basic allergic constitution persists, and the manifestations may later reappear in the skin or upper respiratory passages or in the alimentary tract.

MEDICAL PROGRESS See page 5.

FUTURE GOALS See page 6.

DRUG THERAPY   See page 6.

TESTS   See page 7.

SERVICES

SPECIALISTS   Less than fifty years ago an allergist's practice was limited to the treatment of hay fever and bronchial asthma. The field has been extended into a study of immunology, the science concerned with the body's ability to resist allergy or other diseases by natural or acquired methods.

Pediatricians and general practitioners can assume the responsibility of diagnosing and treating allergies, but may refer patients to an allergist and request a report of his findings.

COMMUNITY HEALTH INFORMATION   County medical societies can furnish names of allergists if there are any in the area. The county medical society may also refer to the nearest hospital handling allergies or respiratory diseases. The address of the local chapter may be obtained by writing or calling the national headquarters of the Allergy Foundation of America, 801 Second Avenue, New York, N.Y., 10017.

HOSPITAL SERVICES   Some hospitals, particularly those with medical school affiliations, have out-patient clinics with facilities for diagnosis, testing, treatment and emergency services for asthma and other allergies.

STATE HEALTH SERVICES   Chronic asthma is treated in almost all state Crippled Children's Programs. However, treatment for other allergies varies widely from state to state.

PRIVATE INSTITUTIONS   In some cases, children with chronic asthma who fail to respond to allergic management may benefit from a change of environment or climate. A list of institutions for asthmatic children is obtainable by writing the Allergy Foundation of America.

FEDERAL RESEARCH
PROGRAMS

The National Institute of Allergy and Infectious Diseases, Bethesda, Maryland, conducts and supports research into the causes, diagnosis, prevention, and treatment of diseases within this classification. See page 201 for a description of recent research.

VOLUNTARY
HEALTH
ASSOCIATION

Allergy Foundation of America
801 Second Avenue
New York, N.Y., 10017

Addresses of local chapters may be obtained by writing or calling national headquarters. There are local chapters in Portland, Oregon; Queens County, New York; Phoenix, Arizona; Plainfield, New Jersey; Meadville, Pennsylvania.

HISTORY OF ASSOCIATION

The Allergy Foundation of America grew out of a need recognized by professional circles and was established by the American Academy of Allergy and the American College of Allergists. It was founded to bring together the public, the medical profession, the research scientists, and public health workers in an effort to solve the problems of allergic diseases.

SERVICES OF NATIONAL HEADQUARTERS

In addition to the responsibility of supervising and supporting programs of research, training, and professional education, the Foundation has national and regional programs to educate the public. Although it does not operate clinics, laboratories, or treatment facilities, it will answer inquiries. The answers to most questions can be found in their printed literature.

Lists of qualified, practicing allergists in any part of the country may be obtained from the Foundation, as well as names of institutions and camps that accept asthmatic children and adults.

SERVICES OF LOCAL AFFILIATES

Chapters furnish information about local facilities for diagnosis and treatment, as well as general information. They also give financial assistance by providing needed equipment for hospitals, for clinics, and for use in the home, under medical supervision. They sponsor physical fitness rehabilitation programs for asthmatic children, public meetings and symposia on all aspects of allergic diseases, and group discussions and workshops for parents. They promote educational activities in local schools dealing with the health problems of asthmatics and severely allergic children and sponsor medical student scholarships. Fundraising activities serve to support local services and help support the public, patient, and physician education program, as well as the research and training fellowship programs of the national organization.

PUBLICATIONS

The Allergy Foundation has the following publications available, if requested in writing:

"Hay Fever"
"Allergy in Children"
"The Skin and Its Allergies"
"Insect Stings"
"Mold Allergy"
"Food Allergy"
"Drug Allergy"
"Answers to Some Questions About Allergy" (free)
"Allergy: Its Mysterious Causes and Modern Treatment"
"Cosmetic Allergy"
"Handbook for the Asthmatic"
"Asthma, Climate, and Weather"
"Allergic Diseases"
"Condensed Annual Reports on Goals and Programs, Activities, and Needs of the Foundation."

EDUCATION With few exceptions, children with allergic diseases attend regular schools. For a list of special institutions for asthmatic children, write to the Allergy Foundation of America.

VOCABULARY

Allergen — A substance which induces an allergic reaction and causes the body to react in a hypersensitive way.

Allergoid — An allergy-producing substance, which, when sufficiently "detoxified," can stimulate resistance to the allergy without causing serious allergy symptoms.

Antibody — A substance, natural or artificial, introduced to serve as protection against infections or other body poisons, or to neutralize their toxins.

Antigen — Any substance which when introduced into the body causes the production of an antibody.

Antihistaminic drugs — Synthetic substances used to alleviate allergic conditions by diminishing the action of histamine.

Histamine — A chemical released by the interaction of the allergen antibody; considered the cause of swelling and itching of allergic skin manifestations.

Hyposensitization — The process of diminishing the sensitivity of an allergy sufferer through injections of the allergen in small doses.

Immunity — A state, natural or acquired, in which the body is resistant to an allergy, or other disease.

Ingestants — Substances which when eaten cause allergic reaction, such as eggs, milk, chocolate, nuts, and shellfish.

Arthritis and Related Rheumatic Diseases

DESCRIPTION OF CONDITION

Arthritis is one of the oldest afflictions of living creatures. Definite evidence of several types of arthritis has been found in Egyptian mummies dating back to 800 B.C., and similar evidence can be seen in fossil remains of reptiles that lived 100 million years ago. The term "arthritis" is derived from the Greek *arthron*, meaning joint, and *itis*, meaning inflammation. It is used loosely for more than eighty forms of rheumatic disease.

The most common rheumatic, or arthritic, diseases are rheumatoid arthritis, osteoarthritis, ankylosing spondylitis, rheumatic fever, and gout. Of all these, rheumatoid arthritis is the most serious—the nation's number one crippling disease. It may appear at any age and as early as infancy. It attacks more girls than boys for reasons not as yet known.

The most common symptom of juvenile rheumatoid arthritis is joint inflammation with pain, fever, soreness, stiffness, and limitation of motion, although other symptoms, such as enlargement of the lymph glands and spleen, may also occur. Fatigue, poor appetite, anemia, weight loss, and muscular weakness are frequent complaints.

An eye disease called iridocyclitis or iritis, the inflammation of the iris, is a serious complication in one out of ten cases of juvenile arthritis. It may lead to cataracts and even result in blindness. Damage may begin before warning symptoms such as redness and pain are apparent. Fortunately, there is a simple, painless eye examination which will detect iridocyclitis in its early stages.

Although no one knows the causes of rheumatoid arthritis, some scientists believe that it may be due to special kinds of tiny viruslike organisms. These "viruses" are distinctive because they lie dormant in the body, perhaps for years,

before suddenly becoming active and causing illness. They are referred to as "latent," which
means hidden or dormant.

Recent research findings indicate that a latent
"virus" may trigger the inflammation of rheumatoid arthritis, setting off a kind of chemical
war within the body, particularly in the joints.
Once activated, the inflammatory process can
become non-stop, an endless chain of chemical
reactions. Experimentation has revealed and de-
coded many of the steps in the chain-reaction
sequence. As more is learned about inflammation
of the joints, researchers hope to find a weak
link in the chain that would be vulnerable to a
drug or drugs that could stop or slow down the
process.

TREATMENT Juvenile rheumatoid arthritis varies in severity and is characterized by unexplained periods
of improvement (remission) and flareups, without warning.

One of the most important developments in
the entire field of arthritis in recent years has
been the realization of how much can be accomplished to help patients with rheumatoid arthritis. Proper rest and exercise; supportive treatment; administration of salicylates, of which
aspirin is one example, and selected drugs; and
sometimes corrective surgery—are all parts of
an effective program. During the treatment the
patient usually is neither hospitalized nor bed-
ridden, and probably not even confined to a wheel
chair. The program is designed to keep the patient in school and as active as possible.

PROGNOSIS There is no cure for rheumatoid arthritis but
serious crippling can be avoided in almost every
instance if treatment is started early and is continuous. Methods of treatment are constantly
improving, and although arthritis is a chronic,
long-term disease it is rarely fatal.

In over half the cases, the joint lesions of juvenile rheumatoid arthritis subside permanently
without residual disability within a few years

or at puberty. Others may develop permanent deformities and some disability before inflammatory activity subsides. In about one-third of the cases the disease continues actively into adulthood.

MEDICAL PROGRESS

Twenty-five years ago it was believed that rheumatoid arthritis was an infectious disease and that it should be treated by eliminating infections. Today scientists are on the verge of solving the mystery of the inflammation and of how and why it goes awry to cause this disease. Once these causes are found, cure and even prevention are foreseeable.

DRUG THERAPY

No drug, at the present time, will cure any form of arthritis, except in the case of infectious arthritis, which can be cured by antibiotics. Based on the needs of the individual patient, physicians may choose various drugs for juvenile rheumatoid arthritis. All medications prescribed are selected for their ability to relieve pain and to control the symptoms of inflammation.

Aspirin is the single most widely used drug in the treatment of juvenile rheumatoid arthritis and was actually developed specifically for the treatment of arthritis. To get its full anti-inflammatory effect, it must be taken in large doses daily, even during periods when pain and swelling have subsided.

SERVICES

SPECIALISTS

A *rheumatologist* specializes in treating the rheumatic diseases, those that affect the supporting or connective tissues of the body. The major disease treated by this specialty is arthritis. With increasing understanding of how immunologic reactions alter the connective tissue structure, rheumatologists have become experts in the allergic and immunologic processes, and have additional knowledge in the fields of rheumatology and allergio-immunology.

A *pediatric rheumatologist* specializes in treatment of children with arthritic diseases, including juvenile rheumatoid arthritis.

An *orthopedic surgeon* is involved in the reconstruction and repair of the functioning of the skeletal system and its associated structures. For some patients with juvenile rheumatoid arthritis, he might perform a *synovectomy*, the surgical removal of an inflamed *synovial membrane.* Tissue around the diseased joint is excised to relieve pain and improve function.

Other health specialists, such as physical therapists and occupational therapists, make important contributions to therapy for the child with juvenile rheumatoid arthritis.

COMMUNITY HEALTH INFORMATION

Local Arthritis Foundation chapters can give information on the nearest facility. See page 18 for address of national headquarters.

The National Easter Seal Society for Crippled Children and Adults, 2023 West Ogden Avenue, Chicago, Illinois, 60612, is the administrative headquarters for the network of some 2,000 Easter Seal affiliates that operate 2,500 direct service programs for handicapped children and adults in every state and in Puerto Rico. They have information on nearest sources of help for arthritic children.

STATE HEALTH SERVICES

State Crippled Children's Programs provide diagnostic evaluative services and treatment for children with juvenile rheumatoid arthritis and related rheumatic diseases. Services provided include: pediatric and orthopedic examination, X-rays, diagnostic tests, surgery, physical therapy supervision, public health nursing services, and nutrition and social service consultations. Treatment facilities and eligibility differ from state to state.

FEDERAL RESEARCH PROGRAM

The National Institute of Arthritis and Metabolic Diseases (NIAMD), one of the National Institutes of Health of the U.S. Public Health Service, was established in 1951. NIAMD supports research in a large number of fields. Its contribution to arthritic programs greatly exceeds that of any other single organization. See page 201 for a description of recent research.

VOLUNTARY HEALTH ASSOCIATION

The Arthritis Foundation
1212 Avenue of the Americas
New York, N.Y., 10036

The Foundation has seventy-six chapters, representing fifty states and the District of Columbia. There are no Foundation affiliates in Alaska, South Dakota, or Wyoming. Chapters are listed in the telephone book as Arthritis Foundation, except in the District of Columbia, where it is listed as Arthritis and Rheumatism Association of Metropolitan Washington, D.C.

HISTORY OF ASSOCIATION

Originally called "The Arthritis and Rheumatism Foundation," the agency was established by a group of physicians and laymen in 1948. Its name was changed in 1964. The following year the American Rheumatism Association merged with the Foundation, becoming its scientific section. In 1967, a new professional society was established as the Allied Health Professions Section of the Foundation, to serve as its liaison with allied medical personnel.

SERVICES OF NATIONAL HEADQUARTERS

The Foundation itself and its seventy-six chapters do not operate research or treatment centers directly. The Foundation offers grants to medical schools, their teaching hospitals or other qualified hospitals or medical institutions to help support clinical research centers.

SERVICES OF LOCAL AFFILIATES

Covering the complete spectrum of total care, including diagnosis, medical treatment, orthopedic surgery, and rehabilitation services, chapters support a great variety of community health services for arthritics, as well as research and clinical research centers and home care programs. Chapters also provide information to the public regarding local treatment facilities.

PUBLICATIONS

Authoritative booklets on the rheumatic diseases are available to the public without charge from local chapters and national headquarters. They include:

"Arthritis—The Basic Facts"

"Rheumatoid Arthritis—A Handbook for Patients"

"The Truth About Aspirin for Arthritis"

"The Truth About Diet and Arthritis"

"Arthritis in Children"

"Arthritis Quackery—A $403,000,000 Racket"

Professional literature and films are available and cover the newest developments in arthritis and rheumatism research and developments for physicians and paramedical personnel.

EDUCATION AND RECREATION Because children with juvenile rheumatoid arthritis suffer irregular flare-ups and remissions and are crippled to such varying degrees, there are no programs, either educational or recreational, specifically set up for them. Moreover, since juvenile rheumatoid arthritis usually "burns itself out" by early adulthood, every effort is made to keep these children in the mainstream of life and activity with normal children. The severely disabled are included in some programs for handicapped children, and those who are homebound are eligible for tutorial and nursing care such as is offered by many state and local boards of education and departments of health.

The Board of Education, Division of Handicapped, the local Arthritis Foundation chapters, and the local Easter Seal Society are all sources of information and guidance.

VOCABULARY

Cartilage —Gristle; a white, semiopaque, nonvascular connective tissue. Joint cartilage is the cartilage covering the joint surfaces of the bones.

Exacerbation —Increase in severity of condition; flare-up.

Remission —Abatement of the symptoms of a disease; the period during which this takes place. Rheumatoid arthritis is a disease in which remissions characteristically take place. Symptoms may subside or disappear completely for unpredictable periods lasting from a few days to a few years, only to return again.

Synovial fluid —The clear fluid, normally present in joint cavities, that lubricates the joint.

Synovial membrane —The inner lining of the capsule surrounding a joint, concerned with secretion of synovial fluid into the joint cavity.

Synovitis —Inflammation of a synovial membrane.

Birth Defects

DESCRIPTION OF CONDITION

The National Foundation–March of Dimes defines birth defects as "structural or metabolic disorders present at birth, whether genetically determined or resulting from environmental interference during embryonic or fetal life."

There are hundreds of birth defects, ranging from gross structural abnormalities—such as open spine—immediately apparent at birth, to subtle errors in body chemistry—such as diabetes—that often go undetected until they cause mental or physical disability in later life.

It is estimated that twenty percent of all birth defects are genetically determined. Another twenty percent are believed to be due to environmental factors, including maternal disease that affects the infant in the uterus. Sixty percent are probably due to the interaction of genetic and environmental influences before birth.

About one in every ten American families has a child with a significant defect. Examples include: mental retardation of prenatal origin, congenital blindness, congenital deafness, genitourinary malformations, muscular dystrophy, congenital heart disease, clubfoot, cleft palate and cleft lip, diabetes, malformations of the digestive system, speech disturbances, cystic fibrosis, sickle cell disease, or hidden defects of body chemistry.

TREATMENT

Many physical and mental disabilities due to birth defects can be completely corrected or reduced in severity by early detection and treatment with the best-known methods of modern medicine.

A single medical breakthrough cannot solve the complex problems and wide variety of birth defects. There is, however, solid scientific conviction that the solution for most is prevention. These are some of the existing programs:

Rubella Vaccine: Now perfected to prevent German measles. Infants whose mothers have the disease during pregnancy suffer severe eye, ear, heart, and other defects.

Rh Vaccine: An injection given an Rh-negative mother after miscarriage, abortion, and birth of each of her Rh-positive babies prevents the build-up of antibodies in the mother's blood-stream that can cause damage to future off-spring. In 1968 the Federal Government licensed an anti-Rh serum which, with universal usage, can eradicate this birth defect that once killed or caused brain damage in 10,000 live-born American babies each year.

Approximately ninety-five percent of live-born babies with Rh disease can be saved by transfusion immediately after birth.

Genetic Counseling: Great progress has been made in the study of chromosomal abnormalities and in the development of ways to identify those who may be carriers of recessive genes. Counseling services have increased, and sound advice is more readily accessible to concerned families and physicians. For physicians an international directory listing genetic services is available through the National Foundation–March of Dimes. A list of counseling services is available to laymen on request.

Fetology: As recently as five years ago, this medical specialty—the diagnosis and treatment of the unborn child—had no name. Today, fetologists study some fetal problems by a method known as "amniocentesis," which means tapping the bag of water surrounding the fetus to obtain cells and chemicals that can give clues to a growing number of defect-causing conditions. Prenatal medication, transfusion, and even surgery have also been accomplished successfully.

Prenatal Care for "High-Risk" Mothers: Women who fall into the category of "high risk" include mothers under eighteen and over forty; mothers with metabolic disorders, such as diabetes and hyperthyroidism; mothers with infectious diseases such as tuberculosis or venereal disease; mothers in parent combinations with

Rh-factor incompatibility who have had a child whose delivery sensitized the mother before the introduction of the new Rh vaccine; mothers who have a history of miscarriages, premature births, or toxemia during previous pregnancies.

MEDICAL PROGRESS The term "birth defects" was unknown fifteen years ago. For laymen the subject was surrounded by ancient superstition. Among scientists the idea of actually doing something about man's inherited traits was considered far fetched. However, medical progress made in the last ten years indicates that this can be a reality. Increased attention has been paid to preventive measures— vaccines, genetic counseling, fetology. Birth defect centers have stimulated an exchange of research findings and the development of methods of early diagnosis, treatment, and evaluation.

While prevention is the ideal, progress in corrective procedures is helping more and more children born with birth defects.

Pediatric Surgery: Great strides have been made in correction of life-threatening structural malformations in the newborn and defects of internal organs. Improved treatment of open spine and water on the brain is saving more lives and permitting better rehabilitation.

Controlling Body Chemistry Defects: Of more than 1,500 different kinds of birth defects, some 100 to 150 are due to metabolic errors. Taken together, they account for mental deficiency, physical disability, or death in tens of thousands of children and adults. It is encouraging that tests for early detection are being perfected, and control by diet or medication is becoming possible for more and more victims of these invisible disorders.

FUTURE MEDICAL GOALS Prevention of birth defects will come with continued research and the dissemination of information on the latest scientific findings on the causes, diagnosis, treatment, and prevention of congenital diseases. This goal will also be furthered by informing the public of advances in medicine and by promoting community service programs for prenatal care and genetic counseling.

TESTS Inborn errors of metabolic processes account for many known kinds of birth defects. Tests for early detection of these errors, such as amniocentesis, are being perfected and can indicate the medication to be administered to control body chemistry.

SERVICES

SPECIALISTS A March of Dimes Birth Defect Center is a concentration of medical professionals. It brings together specialists from many fields to consult with each other, so that all the problems of the children referred to them may be dealt with. At these centers pediatricians, neurologists, orthopedists, surgeons, plastic surgeons, urologists, psychologists, pediatric nurses, physical therapists, medical social workers, and other experts can focus on a single patient during a single visit. Their advice must then be followed by the doctor who refers the patient to the Birth Defect Center, and by the patient's parents who must maintain care at home.

COMMUNITY HEALTH INFORMATION Listed in your telephone directory as The National Foundation-March of Dimes with county chapter listed first.

Local offices of the Department of Health have facilities for treating birth defects or will make referrals to a hospital or state health facility.

STATE HEALTH SERVICES The Crippled Children's Program in each state has facilities for treatment of the following:

Congenital Malformations—Malformations of circulatory system and bones and joints; spina bifida; cleft palate, cleft lip.

Diseases of the Bones and Organs of Movement—Clubfoot, the varieties known as *talipes*

valgus and *talipes varus;* curvature of the spine.
Metabolic Disorders—Diabetes; phenylketonuria.
Congenital Blindness and Deafness—Lesser
visual and hearing impairment.
*Muscular dystrophy, cystic fibrosis, congenital
heart disease,* and *circulatory diseases* are also
treated.

FEDERAL RESEARCH PROGRAM
Several National Institutes of Health are concerned with congenital defects. See page 198 for
a description of responsibilities of each institute.

VOLUNTARY HEALTH ASSOCIATION
The National Foundation–March of Dimes
P.O. Box 2000
White Plains, New York 10602
The Foundation has some 3,000 county chap-
ters throughout the United States. They are list-
ed in the telephone book under The National
Foundation–March of Dimes, (Name of County)
Chapter, or (Name of County) Chapter–The
National Foundation.
Chapters have information on the nearest Birth
Defect Center or March of Dimes Medical Service
Program. A list of genetic counseling services in
the United States and Canada is available to
physicians and others in the health professions on
request from the Professional Education Department, The National Foundation, at the above
address.

HISTORY OF ASSOCIATION
Franklin D. Roosevelt founded the National
Foundation for Infantile Paralysis in 1938 at a
time when it seemed impossible to prevent polio.
The organization led the fight against polio which
resulted in the discovery of the Salk vaccine—
and the possibility of eliminating the disease.
This accomplished, the Foundation decided to
utilize its experience and energy on two long-
neglected but extremely serious public health
problems, arthritis and birth defects. By 1964,
there was justification for the formation of a

separate Arthritis Foundation. The National Foundation now devotes itself solely to birth defects.

SERVICES OF NATIONAL HEADQUARTERS

Primarily supports scientific research and medical science; makes referrals to affiliate facilities; produces and distributes public and professional educational materials. Also sponsors international, national and regional symposia on causes and prevention of genetic disease and other birth defects for practicing physicians and allied health workers.

SERVICES OF LOCAL AFFILIATES

More than one hundred March of Dimes Birth Defects Centers are designed to serve the needs of the community and to work with other local and regional agencies. These centers conduct research to learn more about the causes of birth defects, and to develop methods of earlier and more accurate diagnosis and improved medical, surgical, and rehabilitation techniques. They also offer genetic counseling and education for professionals.

Each center provides teams of specialists for the accurate diagnosis of birth defects; consultation and guidance is offered to local physicians. Some centers provide comprehensive care for inpatients as well as out-patients.

Local chapters are not encouraged to expend funds for patient aid. In certain cases, depending on the availability of funds and advice from their medical advisory committees, local chapters may help meet the cost of necessary treatment when no other resource is open to the patient.

Some chapters sponsor conferences and meetings for concerned parents and other nonprofessionals in the community, to inform them of the nature and severity of birth defects and the progress being made.

They also furnish brochures, exhibits, and films for nonprofessional groups as part of their public education program and serve as a source of information on resources available in the community. Prenatal care clinics and education programs are conducted to make the public aware of preventive measures such as rubella vaccination and the anti-Rh serum.

VOLUNTARY HEALTH ASSOCIATION The National Easter Seal Society for Crippled Children and Adults, 2023 West Ogden Avenue, Chicago, Illinois 60612, is the administrative headquarters for a network of some 2,000 Easter Seal affiliates that operate 2,500 direct service programs for handicapped children and adults in every state and in Puerto Rico. Services are based on the particular needs of communities.

In some centers treatment is given to the following disorders: birth defects, congenital anomalies, orthopedic disorders, and neurological and neuromuscular disorders.

Also treated are speech, hearing, and related disorders; learning disorders; and psychological disorders.

GENETIC COUNSELING

VOLUNTARY HEALTH ASSOCIATION National Genetics Foundation
250 West 57th Street
New York, N.Y. 10019

Foundation offers family counseling and makes referrals through physicians or for individuals to genetic counseling and treatment centers throughout the country.

HISTORY OF ASSOCIATION

The National Genetics Foundation (formerly the National Foundation for Genetic and Neuromuscular Disease), a voluntary nonprofit tax-exempt organization, was initially founded to concentrate a scientific attack on one disease: muscular dystrophy. Because of the close interrelationship between the various diseases that destroy the functioning of the human neuromuscular system, the Board of Directors in 1960 adopted the recommendation of its Medical Advisory Board to support research in these allied diseases as well. The Foundation has now turned its efforts to research into human genetics to discover the causes and the means of treatment of the more than 2,000 known hereditary diseases.

SERVICES OF NATIONAL HEADQUARTERS
The organization is engaged in the following activities:

Operation and support of a genetic counseling and treatment network. Makes referrals through physicians to centers.

Support of basic and clinical research.

Education of physicians on developments in human genetics, with special emphasis on the value and importance of genetic counseling.

Education of the general public in the broad principles of human genetics, with emphasis on the value and importance of genetic counseling from the patient's point of view.

Treatment of genetic diseases.

VOCABULARY

Congenital malformation —A deformity existing at birth due to improper formation of the baby in the uterus; may be due to genetic factors or injury to the embryo early in its life in the uterus.

Down's Syndrome (Mongolism) —A congenital disease accompanied by mental deficiency; some forms are hereditary. Typical facial appearance is marked by broad, flat features, obliquely set eyes and large tongue. Now known to be linked to unusual chromosome patterns in body cells.

Genes —The basic units of heredity, arranged linearly and located at definite points (loci) in a chromosome. They occur in pairs, situated at corresponding loci of a pair of homologous chromosomes. Two types of genes exist: structural genes and operator or regulator genes.

Inborn error of metabolism — Phrase coined for birth defects in which some error in the chemical processing machinery of the body leads to disease or disorder.

Phenylketonuria (PKU) — A hereditary metabolic disease due to inability to metabolize the amino acid phenylalanine. The disease is now readily identified by simple urine tests or blood tests, which have brought many cases to light. Keeping phenylalanine out of diet, if started early, prevents mental retardation and other complications of the disease. Many states have routine PKU tests for all new-born infants.

Blindness
and Partial Sightedness

DESCRIPTION OF
CONDITION Definitions of blindness range from complete
loss of sight to various degrees of residual vision.
The American Foundation of the Blind prefers
that the term "blindness" be reserved for a complete loss of sight, with all other degrees of visual
loss considered as "visual impairment." The latter can be accurately determined by ophthalmic
measurements. Approximately 35,000 children
and young people under twenty-one in this
country are blind.

Most states, however, in determining public
assistance eligibility and income tax exemption,
accept the "legal" definition of blindness: A person is said to be legally blind if he can see no more
at a distance of twenty feet than a person with
normal sight can see at a distance of 200 feet.

People whose visual acuity is 20/70 or less in
the better eye, after the best possible correction,
and who can still read print are referred to as
"partially sighted." According to the National
Society for the Prevention of Blindness, there
are 1,980,000 adults and 148,000 children in the
United States who are unable to read ordinary
print even with the aid of glasses. Only one-fifth
of this group are considered legally blind; the rest
are not, therefore, eligible for many governmental and private agencies whose services are restricted to those falling within the definition of
legal blindness.

The incidence of blindness in infancy was
sharply reduced when it became apparent in the
early 1900's that something was needed to combat the prevalence of ophthalmia neonatorum,
known as "babies' sore eyes". Through the efforts
of the National Society for the Prevention of
Blindness support was finally won to bring about
the use of the prophylaxis, silver nitrate, to be
used in the eyes of all newborn babies. Today

all states but three require its use by law or regulation.

Another cause of blindness in infants was reduced when the relationship of retrolental fibrosplasia to an oversupply of oxygen in the care of premature babies was demonstrated in 1953.

Despite the progress of educational programs designed to serve visually handicapped children, less than 15,000 school children classified as "partially sighted" receive benefits of special education. Less than 10 per cent of school districts in the United States have special educational programs for the partially seeing. It is estimated that as many as 100,000 school children could benefit from large print materials.

The extent and quality of the services provided depend upon the size of the community, the training of the personnel, availability of community resources, and the state educational agency reimbursement procedures.

Standard professional practice in special education is to place and teach visually handicapped children on the basis of the effects the vision impairment has upon the child. However, other factors—motivation, prior learning, intelligence, and experience with special media—can be more relevant than measurements of visual acuity in achieving goals.

The special objectives of education for visually handicapped children are most effective when they include the following:

Efficient Use of Vision—Training in the use of residual vision.

Education Adjustment—Programs are geared to prevent failure; testing and counseling determine the capability of the student.

Social Adjustment—Attempts are made to establish a sense of self-worth and self-respect, and to set personal achievement goals.

Vocational Guidance—The administering of aptitude tests; presentation of appropriate vocational areas; referral to appropriate rehabilitation services.

Only a professional person familiar with the characteristic behavior and skills of a person functioning without sight, such as his use of auditory cues or methods of orientation in a new environment, can appraise and evaluate a youngster's potential.

Because of behavioral problems, some blind or partially sighted children present problems to parents and to professional persons interested in providing educational and social services. These children are considered "multiply handicapped" because of behavioral problems as well as physical handicaps. They are sometimes incorrectly described as being "mentally deficient" because of slow mental development; or as "emotionally disturbed" or "brain damaged" because of the social consequences of their physical condition.

In order for the blind child to benefit from an educational program, perhaps the first efforts must be directed toward helping his parents understand his blindness, their own feelings toward him, and his developmental needs in relation to his visual loss.

The child with a visual loss benefits from his educational and social experiences by gaining an understanding of himself and his needs. In some instances, psychotherapy or "play therapy" may be helpful. The expense, and in some areas the inaccessibility of therapists, may make treatment unavailable for many families.

For some children with behavior problems in addition to their visual handicap, an educational program provided on a residential basis may be indicated.

SPECIALISTS   *Ophthalmologists* are physicians who specialize in diagnosis and treatment of defects and diseases of the eye, performing surgery when necessary or prescribing other types of treatment, including glasses.

An *optometrist* is a licensed, nonmedical practitioner, who measures refractive errors (irregularities in the size or shape of the eyeball or surface of the cornea) and eye muscle disturbances. In his treatment the optometrist uses glasses, prisms, and exercises only.

An *optician* grinds lenses, fits them into frames, and adjusts the frames to the wearer.

STATE HEALTH
PROGRAM

Most states have established either a division within the welfare department or a separate agency of a similar nature to give information on all matters relating to services to blind persons, whether these services are administered by that agency or not.

Services available at the state agencies generally include counseling for parents and education of blind children: communication skills are taught, and in addition children are trained in mobility and given vocational counseling. In some instances, financial assistance is available.

All these services are available throughout the United States, the Virgin Islands, Puerto Rico, and Guam at public and private agencies. The federal government cooperates with the states in a program that stresses rehabilitation.

Special laws passed for the benefit of blind persons provide library materials (braille, large type, and talking books) and privileges such as travel concessions and tax exemptions, and, in some states, financial assistance for education.

For information or assistance concerning a blind child, begin by contacting the governmental agency in the following list which administers the federal-state program.

ALABAMA Vocational Rehabilitation and Crippled Children Service, 2129 East South Boulevard, Montgomery 36111; (205) 269-7571

ALASKA Office of Vocational Rehabilitation, Alaska Office Building, Pouch F, Juneau 99801; (907) 586-3270

ARIZONA Division of Rehabilitation for the Visually Handicapped, Department of Public Welfare, State Office Building, 112 North Central Avenue, Phoenix 85004; (602) 271-4354

ARKANSAS	Rehabilitation Services for the Blind, 900 West Fourth Street, Little Rock 72201; (501) 371-1501
CALIFORNIA	Department of Rehabilitation, 714 "P" Street, Sacramento 95814; (916) 445-3971
COLORADO	Division of Rehabilitation, Services for the Blind Section, State Department of Social Services, 1575 Sherman St., Room 122, Denver 80203; (303) 892-2763
CONNECTICUT	State Board of Education and Services to the Blind, 170 Ridge Road, Wethersfield 06109; (203) 249-8525
DELAWARE	Commission for the Blind, 305 West Eighth Street, Wilmington 19801; (302) 655-4444
DISTRICT OF COLUMBIA	Department of Vocational Rehabilitation, Section for the Visually Impaired, 1331 "H" Street, N.W., Washington 20005; (202) 629-4023
FLORIDA	Department of Health and Rehabilitative Services, Division of Vocational Rehabilitation, Bureau of Blind Services, Charley Johns Building, 725 So. Bronough Street, Room 161, Tallahassee 32034; (904) 222-4398
GEORGIA	Office of Vocational Rehabilitation Services, State Office Building, Atlanta 30334; (404) 688-2390
GUAM	Guam Division of Vocational Rehabilitation, P.O. Box 3009, Agana 96910; 42-4271
HAWAII	Department of Social Services, Division of Vocational Rehabilitation, P.O. Box 339, Honolulu 96809; (808) 507-711
IDAHO	Idaho Commission for the Blind, Sixth and State Streets, Boise 83707; (208) 344-5811
ILLINOIS	Department of Children and Family Services, 404 New State Office Building, 401 South Spring Street, Springfield 62706; (217) 525-7615
INDIANA	Indiana Agency for the Blind, 536 West Thirtieth Street, Indianapolis 46223; (317) 923-3363
IOWA	Commission for the Blind, 524 Fourth Street, Des Moines 50309; (515) 283-0153
KANSAS	Division of Services for the Blind, State Department of Social Welfare, State Office Building, Topeka 66612; (913) 296-3276
KENTUCKY	Bureau of Rehabilitation Services, Division of Services for the Blind, State Office Building, Frankfort 40601; (502) CA 4-2231

LOUISIANA | Division for the Blind, Department of Public Welfare, P.O. Box 44065, Baton Rouge 70804; (504) 389-5962

MAINE | Bureau of Rehabilitation, Division of Eye Care and Special Services, State House, 239 State Street, Augusta 04330; (207) 622-4511, Ext. 548

MARYLAND | Division of Vocational Rehabilitation, 2100 Guilford Avenue, Baltimore 21218; (301) 383-3010

MASSACHUSETTS | Massachusetts Commission for the Blind, 39 Boylston Street, Boston 02116; (617) 727-5580

MICHIGAN | Division of Services for the Blind, Lewis Cass Building, Lansing 48913; (517) 373-2062

MINNESOTA | State Services for the Blind, Department of Public Welfare, 1745 University Avenue, St. Paul 55104; (612) 221-2687

MISSISSIPPI | Rehabilitation Division for the Blind, P.O. Box 4321, Fondren Station, Jackson 39216; (601) 355-9361, Ext. 600

MISSOURI | Bureau for the Blind, State Office Building, Jefferson City 65101; (314) 636-2161

MONTANA | Division of Blind Services, P.O. Box 1723, Tenth and North Ewing Streets, Helena 59601; (406) 449-3434

NEBRASKA | Div. of Rehabilitation Services for Visually Impaired, 2104 "O" St., Lincoln 68510; (402) 473-1681

NEVADA | Services to the Blind Division, 311 North Curry Street, Room 113, Carson City 89701; (702) 882-7415

NEW HAMPSHIRE | Bureau of Blind Services, State House Annex, Concord 03301; (603) 225-6611

NEW JERSEY | Commission for the Blind, 1100 Raymond Boulevard, Newark 07104; (201) 648-3333

NEW MEXICO | Services for the Blind Section, Social & Rehab. Services Dept., State Capitol Complex, PERA Building, Room 317, P.O. Box 2348, Santa Fe 87501; (505) 827-2107

NEW YORK | New York State Department of Social Services, Commission for the Blind and Visually Handicapped, 1450 Western Avenue, Albany 12203; (518) 475-7261

NORTH CAROLINA | Commission for the Blind, Box 2658, Raleigh 27602; (919) 829-4231

NORTH DAKOTA | Division of Vocational Rehabilitation, 418 East Rosser Avenue, Bismarck 58501; (702) 224-2905

OHIO	Bureau of Services for the Blind, Dept. of Social Rehabilitation, 85 South Washington Avenue, Columbus 43215; (614) 469-4272
OKLAHOMA	Dept. of Public Welfare, Sequoyau Memorial Office Bldg., Division of Visual Services, State Capitol Station, Oklahoma City 73123; (405) JA 1-3451
OREGON	Commission for the Blind, 535 S.E. Twelfth Avenue, Portland 97214; (503) 226-2161
PENNSYLVANIA	Dept. of Public Welfare, Bureau of the Visually and Physically Handicapped, P.O. Box 2675, Harrisburg 17120; (717) 787-3582
PUERTO RICO	Dept. of Social Services, Vocational Rehabilitation Division, 1663 Ponce de Leon Ave., Santurce 00910; (809) 723-8010
RHODE ISLAND	Division of Services for the Blind, 46 Aborn Street, Providence 02903; (401) 861-7950
SOUTH CAROLINA	Commission for the Blind, 400 Main Street, Columbia 29201; (803) 758-2595
SOUTH DAKOTA	Service to the Blind and Visually Handicapped, 222 East Capitol Avenue, Pierre 57501; (602) 224-5911, Ext. 318, 319
TENNESSEE	Services for the Blind, Department of Public Welfare, Parkway Towers—Suite 1311, 404 James Robertson Parkway, Nashville 37219; (615) 741-3163
TEXAS	Commission for the Blind, Sam Houston State Office Building, Austin 78701; (512) 475-3811
UTAH	Services for the Visually Handicapped, 309 East First Street South, Salt Lake City 84111; (801) 328-5591
VERMONT	Division for the Blind and Visually Handicapped, 128 State Street, Montpelier 05602; (802) 223-2311
VIRGIN ISLANDS	Insular Dept. of Social Welfare, Division of Vocational Rehabilitation, P.O. Box 630, St. Thomas 00801; (809) 774-2835
VIRGINIA	Commission for the Visually Handicapped, 3003 Parkwood Avenue, Richmond 23221; (703) 770-2181
WASHINGTON	Dept. of Social & Health Services, Div. of Public Assistance, Services for the Blind, 3411 South Alaska Street, Seattle 98118; (206) PA 2-6695

WEST VIRGINIA Vocational Rehabilitation Division, State Capitol Building, Room W-400, Charleston 25305; (304) 348-2375

WISCONSIN Services to the Blind, 5316 West State Street, Milwaukee 53208; (414) 771-5311

WYOMING Services for the Visually Handicapped, Capitol Building, Room 315, Cheyenne 82201; (307) 777-7279

FEDERAL RESEARCH PROGRAMS The National Eye Institute conducts and supports research into disorders of the eye and visual system. For a description of recent research see page 199.

VOLUNTARY HEALTH ASSOCIATION American Foundation for the Blind, Inc.
15 West 16th Street
New York, N.Y. 10011

HISTORY OF ASSOCIATION
In the early part of this century, many people prominent in work for the blind in this country began to think and talk seriously about the need for a national organization devoted to the welfare of blind persons. Although the time was not ripe for formation of such an organization, the idea did not die. In 1921, H. Randolph Latimer, then president of the American Association of Workers for the Blind, agreed to lead a campaign to establish a national organization. The Foundation was incorporated in the State of Delaware "to aid the blind and partially blind of America and to cooperate with any organization, association, institution, or individual engaged in improving the condition of the blind and partially blind."

The Foundation was fortunate in having Helen Keller and Anne Sullivan Macy as enthusiastic supporters from the beginning.

SERVICES OF NATIONAL HEADQUARTERS
The Foundation serves as a consultative organization to local agencies serving blind and partially seeing persons. It also refers individuals to those local agencies from which they can receive direct help. The Foundation itself does not offer ser-

vices directly to blind children, except for the sale of certain specially adapted aids and appliances.

The Foundation carries out an active educational program among teachers, social workers, medical personnel, and others interested in visual disability, as well as among the general public. They publish books, magazines and leaflets in large print and a limited number in Braille form. They also produce phonograph records and tape cassettes.

The Foundation manufactures and sells special aids for use by blind people: games such as Bingo and Scrabble with Braille indications; embossed maps; mathematical aids such as slide rules and protractors; Braille thermometers and postage meters; and clocks and watches with Braille indications.

ADDITIONAL SERVICES

The Foundation does not have affiliates; it does, however, maintain a direct liaison with public and private institutions and agencies serving blind and visually handicapped people. Consultation is provided on all phases of administration, and assistance is given in planning staff development programs.

Regional offices are a referral resource for professional and people needing direct services. Write the Foundation for the addresses of regional offices.

PUBLICATIONS

The Foundation publishes a number of pamphlets. Of particular interest to parents and children are the following:
"Catalog of Aids and Appliances"
"Is Your Child Blind?"
"Some Suggested Sources of Equipment and Teacher Aids for Partially Seeing Children"
"Understanding Braille"

HEALTH ASSOCIATION National Society for the Prevention of Blindness, Inc.

79 Madison Avenue
New York, N.Y. 10016
The Society has affiliated societies in twenty-two states and in Puerto Rico.

HISTORY OF ASSOCIATION
The Society was founded in 1908 to combat the prevalence of *ophthalmia neonatorum*, known as "babies' sore eyes," which was the cause of blindness in twenty-eight percent of all children in schools for the blind.

It was through the efforts of Louisa Lee Schuyler and F. Park Lewis, M.D., a New York physician, and their committee that the support of philanthropists, physicians, and social and business leaders was gradually won to bring about the prophylactic use of silver nitrate in the eyes of all newborn babies.

The Society continues to work in the field of investigative studies of the causes and prevention of blindness.

SERVICES OF THE SOCIETY
The National Society with its state affiliates carries out a comprehensive program of service, education, and research with sole emphasis on blindness prevention. The program includes:

Sponsorship of vision screenings for preschool age children, conducted by specially trained volunteers, to detect eye problems early for best treatment success; guidance on eye safety practices in schools, playgrounds, home workshops, and industry; glaucoma screening for adults.

General public education regarding eye care and health, and eye safety, through literature, films, special workshops.

Financial support of laboratory and clinical research in eye diseases and conditions, causes of blindness, improved methods of diagnosis and treatment.

PUBLICATIONS/FILMS

Available from the national headquarters or from its state affiliates are pamphlets on many aspects of eye health and eye safety. The Catalogue of Publications and Films lists all publications, including:

"Safe Play To Save Sight"
"Charlie Brown, Detective"
"TV and Your Eyes"
"Make Sure Your Child Has Two Good Eyes"

Films for both professional and nonprofessional audiences are available on loan without charge. Vision Testing Charts and educational materials are also available.

NOTE: The Library of Congress receives federal funds to maintain a library for the blind. Some of the materials available are large-print literature, recorded music, and books in the form of Braille, talking records, and tapes. About forty libraries throughout the country serve as regional distributing centers for these materials which can be mailed free of charge. Address inquiries to Division for the Blind and Physically Handicapped, Library of Congress, Washington, D.C. 20542.

VOCABULARY

Amblyopia —Dimness of vision without apparent disease or change of structure of the eye; it arises from an imperfect sensation on the retina, frequently as a result of toxic substances or traumatic experiences.

Cornea —The clear, transparent portion of the outer coat of the eyeball forming the front of aqueous chamber.

Depth perception —The ability to perceive the solidity of objects and their relative position in space.

Diplopia —The seeing of one object as two.

Hemianopsia —Blindness of one-half the field of vision of one or both eyes.

Iris — The colored, circular membrane suspended behind the cornea and immediately in front of the lens. It is the iris which regulates the amount of light entering the eye by changing the size of the pupil.

Lens — A refractive medium having one or both surfaces curved.

Peripheral vision — The ability to perceive the presence, motion, or color of objects outside of the direct line of vision.

Retina — The innermost coat of the eye, formed of sensitive nerve fibers and connected with the optic nerve.

Safety glasses — Impact-resistant glasses, available with or without visual correction.

Snellen chart — Used for testing central visual acuity. It consists of lines or letters, numbers or symbols in graded sizes; each size is labeled with the distance at which it can be read by the normal eye.

Cancer/Leukemia

CANCER

Cancer is rare in children in comparison to other diseases. However, it is fatal to more children between the ages of one and fourteen than any other disease. It ranks second only to accidents in the mortality rate.

The two major classifications of cancers are: *carcinoma*, or malignant growth of epithelial origin (coming from the covering of the skin and linings of various organs); and *sarcoma*, or malignant growths of nonepithelial origin, such as cancer of muscle and nerve tissue, fat or bone. Cancer is actually a group of diseases, for there are as many varieties of cancer as there are organs and tissues in the body.

Most of the tumors that occur in children originate in one of four systems: the nervous system, the genitourinary system, the blood-forming system, and the system of connective tissues, including the bones and muscular structures. The specific organs most frequently attacked are the eye, the brain, the nerve structures lying in the pelvis and behind the abdominal cavity, the kidney, lymph nodes, and bone marrow, and the bones.

Acute leukemia, a cancer of the blood-forming system, is one of the commonest forms of malignant disease in young children. It follows a much more active course than the chronic forms and is likely to progress rapidly in contrast to the slow, insidious onset of leukemia in older people. (See page 48.)

Tumors of the kidney are also among the most frequent of the malignant tumors seen in children. Wilms' tumor, named after the doctor who first described it in detail, can be cured by early treatment in a good many cases.

Neuroblastomas are a common abdominal tumor in children that arise in the fibers of the sympathetic nerve structures behind the abdominal cavity along each side and in front of the spine. These tumors have a tendency to spread early in their growth to the bones, especially those of the spine and skull.

Compared with the incidence of all other kinds of cancer, sarcoma of bone occurs rarely. Yet it is one of the more common tumors in children and young adults. It is found more often between the ages of five and twenty-five than at any other time of life.

Certain brain tumors are encountered as often in children as in adults. Somewhat less common among children's tumors are the sarcomas originating in the soft connective tissues and the tumors that occur in the regions of the head and neck.

TREATMENT
There are only two ways of curing cancer: by completely removing it surgically, or by destroying it with high-energy radiations such as X-rays and the rays given off by radium and some radioactive isotopes like cobalt. Other forms of treatment are used to prolong life. If a cancer is detected early enough, while it is localized and has not spread, surgery and radiation can prove extremely valuable. Developments in surgical and radiation therapy combined with early diagnosis have increased the cure rate. *Chemotherapy* is the treatment of cancer with chemicals which can seek out and destroy specific malignant cells and tissues without harming normal healthy tissues; it has been useful in eliminating pain and prolonging life.

PROGNOSIS
Many cancers can be cured if detected early in their development and treated. The survival rate for cancer patients today is about one in three. It could be one in two by means of early diagnosis and prompt treatment, using techniques that are now available. Unfortunately, a child with cancer may display symptoms not very apparent until it is beyond effective treatment.

MEDICAL PROGRESS
Improved diagnostic procedures, development in surgical and radiation therapy, and chemother-

apy have increased the cure rate. With the recent development of new multimillion-volt X-ray generators and radioactive cobalt-60, many cancers deep within the body which were not previously within the range of radiation therapy may be treated.

FUTURE MEDICAL GOALS
The ultimate goal of cancer research is the discovery of means of preventing or curing this group of diseases. The current emphasis is placed on basic questions concerning the chemistry and biology of growth itself. Further information is sought about the nature of the transformation of cells from normal to cancerous and the biological and biochemical differences between normal and cancerous cells.

TESTS
A *biopsy*, the microscopic examination of a fragment of the tumor, provides the only strictly reliable basis for a diagnosis of cancer. X-ray examination, visualization of the tumor through instruments, and major surgical exploration may also be needed.

SERVICES

SPECIALISTS
Specialists involved in the diagnosis and treatment of cancer patients include *pediatricians*, particularly those who have a subspecialty in cancer; *pathologists* trained in detecting the presence of cancer; *chemotherapists*, who administer radiation therapy; *hematologists*, specialists in the treatment of diseases of the blood, such as leukemia and anemia, and secondary reactions that affect the blood due to such conditions as cancer.

COMMUNITY HEALTH INFORMATION
American Cancer Society has approximately 3,000 units; listed in the telephone book as American Cancer Society.

Leukemia Society of America has more than forty chapters. Check the telephone book or write to national headquarters for nearest chapter. See page 51.

Cancer Care, Inc., provides direct service to all individuals and families living within a fifty-mile radius of New York City. See page 47 for a description of services.

STATE HEALTH PROGRAM Each state either has its own facilities for diagnosis and treatment of children with cancer or makes arrangements with neighboring states.

FEDERAL RESEARCH PROGRAM The National Cancer Institute is one of the research divisions of the National Institutes of Health with funds appropriated annually by Congress. Its support of research throughout the United States and related activities contributes to increased understanding of cancer and allied diseases. See page 199 for a description of recent research.

VOLUNTARY HEALTH ASSOCIATION American Cancer Society
219 East 42nd Street
New York, N.Y. 10017

There are separate incorporated affiliated divisions of the American Cancer Society on a state-wide basis in all fifty states, the District of Columbia, and several metropolitan areas: Philadelphia, Milwaukee, New York City, and Westchester, Nassau, Queens, and Suffolk counties in New York. There are fifty-eight divisions and approximately 3,000 units.

HISTORY OF ASSOCIATION
In the early 1900s it became apparent that if some cancers were detected early and treated promptly they could be cured. But too few were diagnosed in time. A group of doctors and laymen established the American Society for the Control of Cancer in 1913 in an attempt to solve this problem.

In the early thirties the Society concentrated on education of physicians, improvement of diagnostic techniques, and treatment of cancer. In 1937 the Society launched its first public education program. Under new bylaws, the Society became the American Cancer Society, Inc., in 1945, with physicians and laymen equally represented on its board.

Educational and service programs were greatly expanded, and a broad national research program was established. To date the American Cancer Society has invested over $272,000,000 in research.

SERVICES OF NATIONAL HEADQUARTERS
Referral to affiliates; literature.

SERVICES OF LOCAL AFFILIATES
In many communities, depending on local voluntary leadership and funds available, the following services are provided by the American Cancer Society: information and counseling service for patient and family to assist and guide them to full use of community medical and social resources; loan of sickroom necessities, such as hospital beds; and they also supply surgical dressings and provide patient transportation to physicians' offices, hospitals, or clinics for diagnosis and treatment.

Some divisions and units also sponsor home-care programs, including bedside care, through the Visiting Nurse Association or a similar agency.

The American Cancer Society does not operate medical or laboratory facilities, treat cancer patients, or pay physicians' fees. In some localities it does support one or more of the following: assistance by medical social workers in dealing with patient's family and home problems; the supply of medications to patients; medically directed and professionally supervised rehabilitation services. Through cooperation and coordination of existing private and governmental agencies the service program is being expanded.

PUBLICATIONS/FILMS
The Society has an immense variety of publications and materials for the public, physicians, and other professional groups. "Cancer in Children"

is a helpful pamphlet, available free. Local units of the Society have additional publications. A film, "Cancer in Children" is available to professional groups.

VOLUNTARY
HEALTH AGENCY

Cancer Care, Inc.
1 Park Avenue
New York, N.Y. 10016

Cancer Care, Inc., is a voluntary social agency providing counseling and concrete services to self-maintaining patients with advanced cancer and their families living within a fifty-mile radius of New York City. The agency does receive and reply to inquiries from other parts of United States. The agency has two main services: 1) to enable patients with advanced cancer to remain at home as long as is feasible, with optimum comfort, 2) to stabilize family life under the stresses of catastrophic illness.

SERVICES

Counseling service, available to both the patient and the family-members, focuses essentially on problems precipitated or aggravated by the patient's illness and outlook, and the adjustments, social and familial, required by it.

Services the agency helps to pay for include nurses, medical homemakers, housekeepers, transportation to private medical care, and cost of medications.

VOCABULARY

Benign tumor —An abnormal growth that is not cancerous.

Biopsy —Removal of a minute section of tissue for microscopic examination in making diagnosis of disease.

Carcinogenic —Causing cancer.

Chemotherapy —Treatment of disease by chemical substances.

Cobalt treatment —Radioactive treatment, used usually for internal cancer.

Malignant tumor —One that grows, spreads, and threatens life; cancer.

Metastasis —The spread of cancer cells.

Radiation therapy —The treatment of cancer with radiant energy which kills or damages cancer cells.

LEUKEMIA

DESCRIPTION OF CONDITION

Leukemia is commonly thought of as a disease of the blood. Actually, it is a disease of the tissues that produce white blood cells—bone marrow, lymph nodes, and spleen.

Leukemia is a generalized disease, not a local tumor. The tissues involved are those which generally protect the body against bacteria, viruses, and other foreign material. In the leukemia patient, the overproduction of the abnormal white blood cells disrupts the production of red blood cells and interferes with blood clotting. In addition, these abnormal white cells are unable to fight infection, their normal function.

There are two basic types of leukemia:

Acute leukemia—Most often thought of as a disease of children, but can occur at any age. Its course without treatment is rapid and survival time is relatively short, often a matter of months. Now, because of recent medical advances, some patients can survive for two or three years, and five years is no longer extraordinary.

Chronic leukemia—Occurs most frequently in adults. Its course is slower than acute leukemia and survival time is longer, sometimes as much as ten years or more.

TREATMENT

Leukemia cannot be treated surgically. In both types, certain drugs can prolong life far beyond the predictions of twenty years ago. Various chemicals and hormones, and occasionally X-ray treatments, are used.

The first effective drug for acute leukemia,

methotrexate, was not available until 1948. Since then there has been steady progress in the introduction of new drugs to prolong life.

The drug 6-mercaptopurine, developed by George Hitchings, M.D., was introduced in 1951 and has contributed to the success in treatment of acute leukemia.

Super-voltage X-ray therapy is another vital therapeutic means that is effective in reversing the actual leukemia process.

Development of specific drugs creates a need for refinement of the supportive therapy for leukemia patients, such as the specific antibiotic agents that can be exceedingly helpful in controlling infection. Progress has been made in refinement and use of the transfusion theory. The development of platelet transfusions and gamma globulin and other blood products have also been of considerable aid in this treatment.

PROGNOSIS There are at present no known means of preventing this disease. Leukemia cures are rare, but prompt detection and proper treatment can prolong the patient's active life for increasingly longer periods.

The survival time of children with acute leukemia has increased from a period of several months to an average of three years in some cases. There are a number of five-year- and ten-year survivals of patients with acute leukemia. Although these prolonged survivals are minimal, it is now possible to discontinue treatment after a period of seven years and to consider some patients as possibly cured.

FUTURE GOALS If a control can be achieved for one year, it can perhaps be extended later, by new drugs, to five years and eventually indefinitely.

DRUG THERAPY At the present time there are more than eight drugs which can be used one at a time or in combination for the control of acute leukemia in children. Now the median survival following diagnosis is two to three years and almost one-third of the patients will live more than five years following diagnosis. In adults, leukemia is more resistant to treatment.

TESTS Blood tests are made to determine the total red and white blood counts, as well as the amount of hemoglobin. In a bone marrow aspiration test, a sample of red marrow is taken for examination.

SERVICES

SPECIALISTS Leukemia is treated by *hematologists*, physicians with specialized knowledge of blood and blood-forming organs, as opposed to solid cancers, which are managed primarily by *oncologists*, who may either be surgeons or internists with special interest in metastatic disease.

COMMUNITY HEALTH INFORMATION Leukemia Society of America, Inc., has more than forty chapters. Consult the telephone book or write to the national headquarters (211 East 43rd Street, New York, N.Y. 10017) for the address of the nearest chapter.

American Cancer Society has 3,000 units in all fifty states as well as in the District of Columbia and several metropolitan areas: Philadelphia, Milwaukee, New York City, and Westchester, Nassau, Queens, and Suffolk Counties in New York. Consult the telephone book or write to national headquarters (219 East 42nd Street, New York, N.Y. 10017) for a list of services for patients with leukemia.

STATE HEALTH PROGRAM Each state either has its own facilities for diagnosis and treatment for children with leukemia or makes arrangements with neighboring states.

FEDERAL RESEARCH PROGRAM Since October 1955, National Cancer Institute personnel have conducted statistical studies of environmental and other possible cancer-causing factors related to childhood leukemia at a field station of the Institute. See page 199 for a description of recent research.

VOLUNTARY HEALTH ASSOCIATION Leukemia Society of America, Inc.
211 East 43rd Street
New York, N.Y., 10017
Addresses of all chapters may be obtained by writing or calling national headquarters.

HISTORY OF ASSOCIATION
A little less than twenty years ago, the parents and friends of a young man who died of leukemia decided to do something meaningful in his memory. They founded the Robert Roessler deVilliers Foundation to help in the education and welfare of boys and young men who were leukemia victims and to provide financial support to both individuals and institutions for the study of and research into the causes of leukemia, its treatment, and its cure.

Since that time, the Foundation, which was renamed Leukemia Society of America, Inc., in 1967, has made grants for the study of leukemia worth more than $6,000,000.

SERVICES OF NATIONAL HEADQUARTERS
National headquarters conducts the research support program, and public and professional education programs; it makes referrals to local chapters.

SERVICES OF AFFILIATES
More than forty chapters provide the following through their Patient-Aid Program: drugs for care, treatment, and/or control of leukemia; laboratory fees and laboratory and service charges for blood transfusions; transportation of patients to and from treatment centers. It also offers a referral service to advise patients and their families about other sources of aid in the community. Chapters have information on medical specialists in their geographical area; university, private hospital, or clinic and treatment center programs; and paramedical

assistants. Some chapters have parent education programs, run diagnostic and evaluation clinics, and sponsor recreation programs.

See page 45 for services of the American Cancer Society.

VOCABULARY

Granulocyte — A white blood cell formed in bone marrow.

Leukocyte — Any one of the white blood cells.

Lymphocyte — A white blood cell formed in lymphoid tissue throughout the body.

Lymphomas — A term that includes various abnormally proliferative diseases of lymphoid tissues.

Lymphoproliferative disorders — Disorders of the lymphoid tissues in which autoimmune disturbances develop. Here the body reacts against its own tissues, with the result that such conditions as hemolytic anemia, rheumatoid arthritis, and other disturbances occur.

Myeloma — A primary tumor of the bone marrow plasma cells.

Neoplasm — Any new and abnormal growth, as a tumor.

Cerebral Palsy

**DESCRIPTION OF
CONDITION** Cerebral palsy is a condition caused by damage
to the human brain, before, during, or shortly
after birth. Brain damage can result from mal-
development, infection, hemorrhage, injury, or
anoxia. This cerebral dysfunction, marked by
neuromuscular problems, has been written about
since the beginning of recorded history. It was
not until the World War II period, however,
th::t a dedicated physician, Winthrop M. Phelps
of Baltimore, made the distinction between
cerebral palsy and other similar diseases. In
fact, it was Dr. Phelps who first coined the
term: *cerebral* (referring to the brain) *palsy*
(lack of control over the muscles). Although
this seems descriptive enough, it is deceptive.
Cerebral palsy, realistically, is a number of
disorders, classified according to the different
muscle-control centers of the brain that are
affected.

These disorders may interfere with normal
walking, running, or other uses of large muscles,
as well as small muscles needed for writing,
sewing, talking, and other finer skills.

There are three main types of patients: the
spastic individual, who moves stiffly and with
difficulty; the *athetoid*, who has involuntary
and uncontrolled movements; and the *ataxic*,
whose sense of balance and depth perception are
disturbed.

The interruption of sufficient oxygen to the
infant's brain is one of the main causes of cerebral
palsy. This interruption can result from premature separation of the after-birth from the
wall of the uterus, an awkward birth position,
prolonged labor, or interference with the umbili-
cal cord. Premature birth, blood type incompatibility between parents, or an infection of the
mother with German measles or other virus
diseases in early pregnancy can also be causative
factors. The condition is neither hereditary,
contagious, nor progressive.

TREATMENT As there are many types of cerebral palsy, each calls for distinct treatment. The major emphasis in all cases, however, is the day-to-day teaching and stimulation of skills that will assist the child in normal growth and development.

Prior to treatment the assets and liabilities of each child must be evaluated by professionals from many fields. Pediatricians, neurologists, orthopedists, social workers, psychiatrists, dentists, and physical, occupational and speech therapists can help to establish the potential of the child and permit the prescription of an individual course of treatment.

Programs are flexible but have certain common ingredients. Most children benefit from physical and occupational therapy which offer combined play and exercise to teach the child early how to relax his muscles and have them respond to his needs. Today children with cerebral palsy are encouraged to enter into group activities and competitive games with other handicapped or normal children; there is an attempt to give them stimulating experiences and encourage their active participation. For some the field of medicine has additional help to offer. Physicians have used drugs effectively in certain cases to reduce muscle spasms and convulsions. Orthopedic surgery has greatly helped others.

Speech and hearing are a major target of treatment in the early years because they affect learning. Developmental centers and nursery schools lay the groundwork for learning experiences, preparing the child either for special education classes or graduating him into the normal school curriculum.

PROGNOSIS Statistics show that if a child with cerebral palsy lives past the infectious diseases of childhood and is able to combat respiratory infections aggravated by an inactive or sedentary life, then life expectancy differs little from the norm.

New scientific developments, new methods and approaches to the nervous system and muscle problems, and new educational and vocational opportunities have brought hope of eventual nearly normal functioning to many more persons than formerly.

MEDICAL PROGRESS   As recently as fifteen years ago little was being done about diseases and disorders of the brain and nervous system because the outlook appeared hopeless. In light of this, recent gains must be viewed as dramatic. Many causes of cerebral palsy have been discovered and preventive steps taken. Routine tests now are made on pregnant women to determine blood compatability with their husbands. If the Rh factor is present, exchange transfusion at birth protects the baby. Immunization against German measles virus, which accounts for many malformed babies, is an exciting advance of the past few years.

Prevention of premature birth is known to be a factor in reducing the chance of brain damage, and improvement in the methods of care of the premature infant is of course another measure of prevention.

The development and standardization of a series of tests for handicapped children have helped teachers to evolve accurate, realistic educational goals for cerebral palsied children with difficulty in communication and locomotion.

FUTURE MEDICAL   The future goals in this field are to delineate,
GOALS   clarify, and identify causes; develop methods for preventing damage; and improve and continually evaluate treatment and management of the persons with cerebral palsy.

TESTS   *Subdural tap*—To determine if there is an accumulation of blood or other fluid between the skull and brain.

Spinal tap—A specimen of fluid is taken from the filled space encircling the spinal cord for microscopal and chemical examination. Infections of the brain and/or spinal cord, tumors, and bleeding may be diagnosed with this technique.

Electroencephalogram (EEG)—Amplifies the electrical rhythms put out by the brain so that they may be recorded and measured. Variations from normal rhythms indicate a tendency toward seizures, tumor, blood clot, and brain damage. (Unfortunately an EEG may show a normal rhythm when any of these diseases or abnormalities are present.)

Pneumoencephalogram—A special X-ray of the skull is taken to determine whether or not there is a tumor, blood clot or diseased brain tissue.

DRUG THERAPY Drugs are needed as muscle relaxants for spasticity; other muscle relaxants are administered for rigidity and tremor. Anticonvulsants are used to control seizures. Stimulants have a paradoxical calming effect on some minimally brain-damaged children and are used to reduce hyperactivity. Tranquilizers are used to help relieve muscle tension and reduce anxiety.

SERVICES

SPECIALISTS Neurologists, pediatricians, psychiatrists, psychologists, orthopedists, nurses, physical therapists, occupational and speech therapists, and dentists are members of the professional team important in the care, training, and management of persons with cerebral palsy. Special education teachers are responsible for particular educational needs.

COMMUNITY HEALTH INFORMATION United Cerebral Palsy, listed in the telephone book, has facilities for treatment and referral services.

STATE HEALTH SERVICES All states include in their Crippled Children's Programs services for those with cerebral palsy. The professional staff of such a service can include an orthopedist, speech pathologist, dentist, physical therapist, and a medical-social worker to help parents with emotional, social, or financial problems.

FEDERAL RESEARCH
PROGRAM

The National Institute of Neurological Diseases and Stroke and the National Institute of Child Health and Human Development support research into the problems of cerebral palsy. See page 203 for a description of recent research.

VOLUNTARY
HEALTH
ASSOCIATION

United Cerebral Palsy Association, Inc.
66 East 34th Street
New York, N.Y. 10016

Hundreds of centers have been set up by the 300 UCP local affiliates across the country.

HISTORY OF ASSOCIATION

United Cerebral Palsy Association, Inc., officially came into being under the membership corporation laws of the State of New York in 1949. The association was founded primarily by parents of cerebral palsied children for the purpose of attacking all phases of the problem. The organization was formed to promote research, treatment, education, and rehabilitation of individuals with cerebral palsy and to subsidize professional training programs.

SERVICES OF NATIONAL HEADQUARTERS

Primarily deals in guidance and services to affiliates; conducts demonstration projects, assesses affiliates' programs, supplies public and professional educational materials, underwrites research and professional training. The Foundation supports extensive medical research programs.

SERVICES OF LOCAL AFFILIATES

Services include medical nursing care, physical and occupational therapy, vocational guidance, home services, sheltered workshops, dental care, psychological counseling, recreation, social programs, day-care centers, preschool classes, speech therapy, parent education, and educational materials.

PUBLICATIONS

Public information literature includes:
"Cerebral Palsy—More Hope Than Ever"

"Cerebral Palsy—What You Should Know About It"
"Two Kinds of Measles—Two Vaccines for Prevention"
"Questions and Answers About Cerebral Palsy"
"Cerebral Palsy—Hope Through Research"
"What Are the Facts About Cerebral Palsy?"
A list of professional literature is available on request.

EDUCATION
Some UCP affiliates have preschool and elementary school classes. Local Boards of Education have information on special classes.

RECREATION
Day camps, day-care centers, and social and psychological recreational programs are offered by some UCP affiliates. Concerned Youth for Cerebral Palsy members work with young people in recreation and social activities. Ys and Boy Scouts and Girl Scouts also have special programs occasionally.

VOCABULARY

Ataxic —No balance, jerky movements; characteristic of one type of cerebral palsy.

Athetoid —Uncontrolled and continuous movements; characteristic of one type of cerebral palsy.

Flexion —Bending, as of elbows, hips, knees, etc.

Hemiplegia —Paralysis of one side of the body.

Paraplegia —Paralysis of the lower limbs.

Quadriplegia —Paralysis affecting the four extremities of the body.

Spasm —Tightening of muscles; characteristic of one type of cerebral palsy.

Cooley's Anemia

DESCRIPTION OF CONDITION

DESCRIPTION OF CONDITION

Cooley's anemia is the name commonly used to describe the severe form of a hereditary disease of the blood mostly found in persons of Italian, Greek, Lebanese, or Chinese origin. It is, however, a universal disease with carriers in many countries. The disease, also called "Mediterranean anemia" or thalassanemia, is inherited; and it is currently believed that the severe form *(thalassanemia major)* occurs in a child born of parents both of whom must be carriers of the trait. There are about 200,000 cases in the United States of *thalassanemia major* and *minor*.

The life of normal red blood cells is measured in months; these cells are continuously replaced by new ones. In Cooley's anemia the red blood cells are abnormal and their survival is often measured in days and weeks.

Thalassanemia major usually becomes manifest during the first year of life and is a fatal disease. Both sexes are equally affected. As a result of the chronic state of anemia, children with this disease are greatly handicapped. Bone growth is poor, and children are usually small for their age. Because of abnormalities of the bone marrow there are alterations of the skull and other bones, so that a characteristic facial expression is found which gives many of these children the appearance of being related. The anemia causes fatigability; nosebleeds are common; and, when anemia is severe, low-grade fever may be noted.

Individuals with the trait or minor form of the disease are not handicapped physically in any significant way; the only detectable manifestation may be changes in size and shape of the red blood cells. Individuals with *thalassanemia minor* have a normal life span and enjoy normal health. The trait does not generally increase in severity or convert to the severe form of Cooley's anemia.

TREATMENT

At the present the only effective treatment is the regular administration of blood transfusions to alleviate the constantly recurring anemia. There are other specific treatments for complications. Specific food substances or vitamins other than those required for a normal balanced diet do not in any way beneficially alter the basic disease.

The frequency of transfusion depends upon the severity of the disease. Some children require blood transfusions as often as once a week and others rarely need them.

MEDICAL PROGRESS It is now possible, because of advances in blood disease research, to determine the presence of Cooley's anemia shortly after birth. Fetal hemoglobin, which is present in all children at birth, normally disappears within the first year of life. However, it remains present in large quantities in children with Cooley's anemia. A special apparatus detects this type of hemoglobin. Similarly it is possible to determine if parents have the traits and may be possible carriers of the disease.

Fifteen years ago, children with the severe form of Cooley's anemia lived until their early teens; today, their life span is extended to their late teens and even beyond. There are rare cases of patients surviving into their thirties.

SERVICES

SPECIALISTS Pediatricians and hematologists are specialists concerned with Cooley's anemia. Basic research into the disease is conducted by geneticists, biologists, and biochemists.

COMMUNITY HEALTH INFORMATION Write to Cooley's Anemia Blood and Research Foundation for Children, Inc., 3366 Hillside Avenue, New Hyde Park, New York, N.Y. 11040.

STATE HEALTH PROGRAM See pages 192–196 for a list of agencies administering health programs for handicapped children. No specific program is available for Cooley's anemia in most states; the agencies, however, can make referrals to the nearest facilities.

VOLUNTARY HEALTH ASSOCIATION

Cooley's Anemia Blood and Research Foundation for Children, Inc.
3366 Hillside Avenue,
New Hyde Park, New York, N.Y. 11040
   Eleven chapters are located in the New York area, New Jersey, Illinois, Pennsylvania, California, Tennessee, and Connecticut.

HISTORY OF ASSOCIATION
In 1954, a small group of interested people found that very little research was being done on Cooley's anemia because of lack of funds. They incorporated under New York State laws and dedicated their efforts to stimulate interest and raise money for the treatment and cure of Cooley's anemia and other blood diseases.

SERVICES OF FOUNDATION
The purposes of the Foundation are twofold. First, they maintain and distribute a blood credit program. This is accomplished through cooperation with the American Red Cross and the National Clearing House Program of the American Blood Bank Association, and other blood banks. Blood accounts are maintained by constant blood procuring programs conducted by members in various localities and by the endeavors of various organizations and industries. These solicitations of blood are disbursed to children with Cooley's anemia, at no cost, to their respective hospitals. As its secondary functions, the foundation promotes means of obtaining funds for the blood credit program and for support of research programs, and publicizes the nature of the disease and the needs of these children.

SERVICES OF AFFILIATE CHAPTERS
Referral to hospital facilities; furnishing supplies of free blood to anyone with Cooley's anemia throughout the country, as well as wheel chairs, beds and other sickroom needs.

PUBLICATIONS/FILMS
Literature dealing with aspects of the handicap is available. A new film, "Another Tomorrow for Teresa," is available free of charge.

VOCABULARY

Erythrocyte —A red blood cell.

Fetal hemoglobin —An oxygen-carrying substance found in red blood cells normally present at birth in large amounts, but disappears in about one year. This hemoglobin is present in abnormally high concentration in Cooley's anemia throughout life.

Folic acid —A substance found in green leaves, liver, and yeast, it is used clinically in treating certain types of anemia.

Liver —The largest gland or organ in the body, it lies in the right upper part of the abdomen immediately under the diaphragm. Functions of the liver are multiple, including secretion of bile, protein breakdown, storage of glycogen and fat, maintenance of composition of blood, and detoxification. Together with the spleen, the liver causes the enlargement of the abdomen and gives the characteristic physical configuration found in patients with Cooley's anemia.

Cystic Fibrosis

DESCRIPTION OF
CONDITION
Cystic fibrosis is the most serious genetic disease affecting the lungs and digestive system of children. Approximately one out of every 1,500 babies is born with the condition, the result of both parents carrying the cystic fibrosis gene. It is believed that one of every twenty persons is a cystic fibrosis carrier—about ten million people. In this hereditary disorder certain glands do not function properly, an abnormally thick mucus is secreted, and sweat glands produce unusually salty sweat. Mucus clogging the lungs causes breathing difficulties and paves the way for infections leading to bronchitis and pneumonia. The lungs may suffer permanent damage. The mucus also interferes with digestion by preventing the flow of enzymes from the pancreas into the small intestine.

The name "cystic fibrosis of the pancreas" was first applied to the disease, now usually known simply as cystic fibrosis, by Dr. Guido Franconi in Switzerland in 1936. Subsequent confirmation of the disorder as a distinct entity was made by Dr. Dorothy Andersen in New York City in 1938.

Symptoms may include a persistent cough, rapid breathing and sometimes wheezing, failure of a baby to gain weight despite excellent appetite, foul-smelling stools, and sweat that is salty to the taste.

TREATMENT
The child may appear to be suffering from asthma, bronchitis, celiac disease, or an allergy. In fact, much of the treatment for cystic fibrosis is the same as for these various other conditions. Research conducted in connection with cystic fibrosis has made possible tremendous improvement and often cure for these other problems.

In some cystic fibrosis-affected children improvement after treatment may be so marked that parents may doubt that their youngster ever had the disease. The child's response may depend to a great extent, however, on how advanced and severe the condition was when treatment was started. Because of variations in the course of the disease and its intensity, treatment is individualized depending on the patient's condition.

In general, the intestinal problems are easily managed by the prescription of extracts of animal pancreas taken with meals to supply the enzymes for digestion.

To prevent or combat lung infections, children may take antibiotics, either by mouth or by inhaling them through an aerosol mask in mist form.

Frequently youngsters benefit from sleeping in plastic tents into which a mist of water is continuously pumped by a compressor or pump installed in the home. This treatment helps to thin the viscous mucus.

Although a child cannot outgrow cystic fibrosis, intensive care and regular follow-up can lead to a relatively normal life. Children with cystic fibrosis often have excellent school attendance records and many are able to participate in games and some sports. Physical activity, determined by the child's tolerance and inclination, is encouraged, with guidance from a physician.

A child with cystic fibrosis is given the usual protective immunization and the same foods as a normal child, with the possible exception of hard-to-digest fats.

PROGNOSIS Only a dozen years ago, most babies with cystic fibrosis died before reaching school age. With today's greater medical and public awareness of the disease, more children are diagnosed earlier and receive appropriate treatment before serious lung damage has occurred. Improvements in the therapy itself also contribute to a brighter outlook. There are now many teen-agers and young adults with cystic fibrosis in college or holding jobs. An increasing number are leading relatively normal lives. Meanwhile, research seeks a control for the condition.

MEDICAL PROGRESS The nebulizer, new antibiotics, and mucus-thinning chemical agents extend the range of treatment possibilities. Some doctors believe that emphasis on *prophylaxis* (treatment intended to prevent complications, as distinguished from treatment begun after they appear) keeps patients in better health.

The average life span of children with cystic fibrosis has been steadily lengthened in recent years.

FUTURE MEDICAL GOALS Work is now progressing on testing methods to detect carriers of the gene before they have children, and to determine prenatally whether cystic fibrosis is present. The knowledge gained from this research will contribute to elimination of the disease.

The nature of the defect is unknown. If the disorder proves to be due to the absence of or faulty functioning in an essential enzyme, enzyme substitution therapy might afford an effective control for the condition — once the precise deficiency is identified.

A practical method of screening every infant to detect cystic fibrosis at the earliest possible moment is another goal toward which researchers are working.

DRUG THERAPY Many drugs, medications, and testing methods are in current use. A solution of propylene glycol and distilled water is commonly *nebulized* (delivered in mist form) for overnight inhalation. Also chemicals and antibiotics are nebulized in small amounts for short treatments at frequent intervals (ten to fifteen minutes, two or four times a day). Pancreatic enzymes, antibiotics, broncho-dilators, and vitamins are all part of the therapy but vary from patient to patient.

TESTS A very reliable test for the disease is the measurement of the salt content of sweat, which is obtained by stimulating a small area of the skin with local heat or chemicals. An excessive amount of salt in the sweat supports the diagnosis of cystic fibrosis. In no other disease with which cystic fibrosis could be confused is there as much salt.

A doctor also needs to know the child's history of digestive and breathing difficulties, or infections and failure to gain weight. A chest X-ray is usually taken initially to determine whether there has been lung damage. The doctor will generally be able to arrive at a diagnosis after he has the whole history and the results of tests taken. If the diagnosis is positive, the disease may be mild or severe, and the degree of pulmonary and gastrointestinal involvement varies with each child.

SERVICES

SPECIALISTS

Specialists involved in treatment in Cystic Fibrosis Centers throughout the country include pediatricians, pulmonary physiologists, roentgenologists, physical therapists, cardiologists, and gastroenterologists.

COMMUNITY
HEALTH
INFORMATION

The National Cystic Fibrosis Research Foundation has chapters or representation to handle all fifty states and the District of Columbia. The nearest chapter will give the address of a Cystic Fibrosis Center. The Foundation is listed in the telephone book under the name of the state or county Cystic Fibrosis Chapter or Association and under Cystic Fibrosis.

STATE HEALTH
PROGRAM

Forty-four states offer exemplary services for cystic fibrosis through clinic services. Services may include diagnosis, medical supervision, hospitalization, provision of drugs, physical therapy, public nurse follow-up, and social services where available for those qualified by the state.

The Crippled Children's Program in most states offers assistance to low income families to offset the cost of drugs, diet supplements and home-care equipment, which often exceeds $1,000 annually, year after year.

FEDERAL RESEARCH PROGRAM

The National Institute of Arthritis and Metabolic Diseases conducts research into the causes, prevention, diagnosis, and treatment of the various arthritic, rheumatic and collagen diseases, and metabolic diseases. Recent research has yielded new insights into the cause of cystic fibrosis. See page 201.

VOLUNTARY HEALTH ASSOCIATIONS

National Cystic Fibrosis Research Foundation, 3379 Peachtree Road, N.E., Atlanta, Georgia 30326.

There are 117 official NCFRF chapters with some 200 branches in forty-eight states and the District of Columbia (they are absent in Delaware and North Dakota which are handled by chapters in other states). Write to national headquarters for information about chapters and their location.

HISTORY OF ASSOCIATION

A concerned group of parents of children with cystic fibrosis and several dedicated physicians created the National Cystic Fibrosis Research Foundation in 1955 as a national, nonprofit, voluntary association. The Foundation has set as its main tasks research; seeking improved treatment; and, ultimately, control or prevention through understanding of the genetic abnormality in the disease.

In 1961 the Foundation began to set up a coast-to-coast network of 110 Cystic Fibrosis Centers staffed by physicians and technicians specially trained in providing home and hospital care for children with lung diseases. Many centers are in hospitals associated with medical schools and are engaged in research and teaching, in addition to diagnosis and treatment.

In April of 1969 the Board of Trustees of the Foundation officially approved broadening medical objectives to include benefits for patients with lung-damaging diseases with symptoms similar to cystic fibrosis. Many children with related diseases are now beneficiaries of the work done by Cystic Fibrosis Center physicians.

SERVICES OF NATIONAL HEADQUARTERS
The national headquarters coordinates and funds Foundation programs for research, education and care. It refers inquiries to their local chapters and Cystic Fibrosis Centers.

SERVICES OF LOCAL AFFILIATES
The chapters throughout the country raise the funds that support the various programs of the National Cystic Fibrosis Research Foundation.

Patient-service programs of local chapters sometimes have equipment pools from which parents may borrow. They frequently perform other services, such as arranging for teachers to visit homebound children or providing transportation for those needing checkups or treatments. They further provide assistance in obtaining drugs at reduced prices and advice as to where special services through clinics and other institutions are available.

Some local chapters have parent-education programs and refer parents to community services for home nursing, treatment facilities, and assistance available from private and public agencies, especially through the State Crippled Children's Service Program.

Chapter Information Programs assume the responsibility of providing speakers, pamphlets, publications, and films designed to increase public awareness and interest in cystic fibrosis.

PUBLICATIONS
Publications available to the layman include the following:

"Parents' Handbook: Your Child and Cystic Fibrosis"

"Directory of Cystic Fibrosis Care, Teaching, and Research Centers"

"Teacher's Guide: A Cystic Fibrosis Child Is in Your Class"

"Living with Cystic Fibrosis: A Guide for the Young Adult"
Professional educational materials available offer detailed information on all aspects of the disease and are distributed to physicians, senior medical students, auxiliary medical personnel, and medical libraries.

EDUCATION Children with cystic fibrosis attend regular schools, subject to absences caused by respiratory infection. Where such service exists and is required, teachers for the home-bound are provided.

RECREATION The chapters also are often a source of information on community recreational facilities. Chapters often conduct social programs for teenagers and adults.

VOCABULARY

Cor pulmonale —A serious heart condition, secondary to the disease in the lungs and/or the blood vessels in the lungs, characterized by a state of elevated pressure in the pulmonary artery which causes strain on the heart.

Pancreatic enzymes —Chemical substances secreted by the pancreas which break down complex food substances into simpler structures which can be absorbed by the intestine. Examples are trypsin, which breaks down or digests protein; lipase, which aids in the digestion of fats; and amylase, which acts on sugars.

Portal hypertension —Abnormally increased blood pressure in the system of veins to the liver, a result of cirrhosis due to increased pressure which is secondary to pulmonary hypertension.

Pulmonary hypertension —Elevated blood pressure in the pulmonary artery system within the lungs.

Deafness/Partial Hearing

DESCRIPTION OF CONDITION

One out of every ten people has some degree of hearing loss—an estimated twenty million Americans. The incidence of hearing loss is increasing due to the fact that advanced medical techniques are prolonging the lives of old people into the age when hearing loss is almost certain to be present. In addition medical advances are saving the lives of many multiply-handicapped (and deaf) children. The development of the German measles (rubella) vaccine is one of the greatest medical steps toward the prevention of deafness in infants.

The most prevalent types of hearing loss are:

1. *Conductive hearing loss:* Eustachian tube dysfunction usually associated with adenoid growth and/or allergic conditions of the nose and sinuses; bony abnormalities which interfere with the normal movement of the *ossicles* (bones of the middle ear).

2. *Sensorineural hearing loss:* Prenatal neural damage or developmental defects may be due to Rh incompatibility, virus infections of the mother (such as German measles) during the first trimester of pregnancy, or infection of the newborn infant by the same virus. Other causes are: *anoxia* (oxygen deficiency) or brain damage at the time of delivery; the effects of some drugs; and prolonged exposure to excessive noise.

MAKE A LINE

TREATMENT

When loss of hearing is due to infection, the physician immediately attempts to stop the progress of the infection and to prevent recurrences.

Ear specialists give a number of highly technical tests which determine the exact degree of deafness, and whether the use of a hearing aid is indicated.

Tests also determine the type of hearing aid best suited to the individual. The two most frequently used types function either by air conduction or by bone conduction.

EDUCATION When *amplification* (the use of a hearing aid) does not correct the hearing problem, special education programs in communication are needed. During the past decade some schools have attempted a Total Communication approach. Total Communication means the use of all forms of communication available to develop language competence. These include: child-devised gestures, speech, formal signs, fingerspelling, speechreading, reading, and writing. This approach, as well as other methods that may be developed in the future, will enable the deaf child to communicate intelligibly with the hearing world.

Where there is a suspicion of hearing impairment, due to genetic or other causes, early testing of an infant is recommended.

For nonreversible hearing impairment, early education in use of speech, speechreading, and hearing aids for use of those with residual hearing will enable the deaf child to learn to read, write, and communicate intelligibly with his family, friends, and the hearing world.

Nursery schools and special preschool classes for the hard-of-hearing and residential schools and special classes in regular schools are part of a comprehensive program of education and rehabilitation for those with defective hearing. For state programs see pages 192–196. For private and public facilities contact health associations listed in this chapter.

NOTE: If there is no nursery class for hard-of-hearing or deaf children in your community, you can write for instruction in the *oralist method* (that is, the use of speechreading rather than the use of signs) to John Tracy Clinic Correspondence Course, 806 West Adams Boulevard, Los Angeles, California 90007.

COMMUNITY HEALTH INFORMATION

State departments of health and the Bureau of Education for the Handicapped will supply information about services and facilities in the state. The local Department of Health is another good source. Information can also be obtained from the health associations listed in this chapter.

A list of schools and classes for the deaf can be found in the directory issue of *The American Annals of the Deaf.* This publication is available in libraries, or can be ordered for $5.00 by writing to: *American Annals of the Deaf,* The Convention of American Instructors of the Deaf, 5034 Wisconsin Avenue, N.W., Washington, D.C. 20016. It also lists clinics, organizations, and publications and gives information about current research.

STATE HEALTH SERVICES

Services for children with hearing impairments vary greatly from state to state. They include: diagnostic services for children with hearing, speech, or language disorders; hearing aids and auditory training in their use; repair of hearing aids and replacement of accessory parts; medical treatment of otologic conditions related to impairment of hearing.

State and local school officials and local health agencies work jointly in hearing conservation. Generally programs consist of early identification of hearing problems and referral for diagnosis, treatment, and rehabilitation.

The Easter Seal Society for Crippled Children and Adults has treatment in some centers for speech, hearing, and related disorders. The Society is listed in local telephone directories. See page 27 for a description of the organization.

FEDERAL RESEARCH PROGRAM

The National Institute of Neurological Diseases and Stroke is responsible for research on the causes, prevention, diagnosis, and treatment of neurological, sensory, and communicative disorders. See page 203 for a description of some recent research.

VOLUNTARY HEALTH ASSOCIATION

National Association of the Deaf
905 Bonifant Street
Silver Springs, Maryland 20910
The Association has forty-one state affiliates.

HISTORY OF ASSOCIATION

In 1880 the National Association of the Deaf was founded by a group of deaf men to protect the rights and privileges of the deaf. Until 1958, the Association operated on a voluntary basis out of the home of its officers. National headquarters was established in 1958 in Chicago, subsequently moved to California, and in 1964 moved to the Washington, D.C., area where it has remained.

SERVICES OF NATIONAL HEADQUARTERS

The Association of the Deaf serves the deaf of all ages, although generally services are directed toward those whose hearing loss began at an early age.

It works for improved educational opportunities and facilities; increased employment opportunities and the removal of discriminatory practices; helps recruit personnel for professional training in areas relating to the deaf; and serves as an information and referral center. It does not concern itself with the medical aspects of deafness other than to serve as a source of reference in medical research.

SERVICES OF AFFILIATES

Referral services to speech and hearing clinics, schools for the deaf, rehabilitation services, state associations for the deaf, and mental health services, as well as providing information for researchers on the characteristics of persons with severe hearing losses and their abilities and employment and socioeconomic status—these are among the services the association provides.

PUBLICATIONS

The Association publishes such helpful pamphlets as:

"Language and Education of the Deaf"
"Deafness and Minority Group Dynamics"
"Training Opportunities—A Guideline for Professionals, Deaf Persons, and Parents"
"A Basic Course in Manual Communication"

A complete list of current publications can be obtained from the Association's headquarters, free of charge; films can be rented from the headquarters for $1.00 each, plus shipping charge.

EDUCATION ASSOCIATION

Alexander Graham Bell Association for the Deaf, Inc.
1537 35 Street, N.W.,
Washington, D.C. 20007

This oralist organization has three sections all at the above address: The International Parents' Organization (for organized groups of parents of hearing-impaired children); the Oral Deaf Adults Section; the American Organization for the Education of the Hearing Impaired (for professionals working with the deaf). It maintains no clinics or treatment centers, but refers those who inquire to the appropriate clinic, treatment center, or school.

HISTORY OF ASSOCIATION

In 1887 The Volta Bureau was founded by Dr. Alexander Graham Bell to disseminate information on all subjects relating to deafness. In 1890, Dr. Bell and his associates founded the American Association to Promote the Teaching of Speech to the Deaf. Known later as the Volta Speech Association for the Deaf, the name was officially changed to the present one in 1953.

SERVICES OF NATIONAL HEADQUARTERS

The Association continues to serve researchers, parents and teachers of the deaf, and others who seek information relating to education and rehabilitation. The Association stresses the importance of the early detection of hearing loss and the beginning of education for those sustaining such loss, particularly the attainment of oral skills by these children.

SERVICES OF LOCAL AFFILIATES
Various local parents' groups, which are affiliates of the International Parents' Organization, offer opportunities for parents to discuss their problems and to formulate plans for improved education for the hearing impaired.

PAMPHLETS/FILMS
The Association has information kits for parents of deaf children and adults; a lending library for members of the association; a library at headquarters for use by researchers, parents, and others interested in the subject. Films for professional and nonprofessional audiences are available.

The Volta Review, the official journal of the Association, is published nine times a year and is sent to all members. Since 1899 it has been the only international publication devoted to modern educational methods of teaching deaf children through the use of speech, speechreading, and residual hearing.

Speaking Out is a newsletter sent to all Association members and to parents who are members of groups affiliated with the International Parents' Organization. The Association's nonprofit publications program concentrates on books and pamphlets relating to modern methods for hearing impaired children and adults. Selected books of other publishers are also handled by the Association as a public service to teachers and parents.

VOLUNTARY HEALTH ASSOCIATION National Association of Hearing & Speech Agencies
919 18 Street, N.W.
Washington, D.C., 20006

HISTORY OF ASSOCIATION
Established over fifty years ago as the American Hearing Society, the name was changed in 1966 to the present one. The purpose of the association is to assist and represent its members in the promotion of high standards of professional service. Affiliated with the national association are 169

member agencies where a person with hearing or speech difficulties can receive some or all of the following services: diagnosis and evaluation, pre-school hearing instruction, counseling and guidance, rehabilitation, and recreational activities.

SERVICES OF NATIONAL HEADQUARTERS
The association makes referrals to member affiliates and conducts public education campaigns through publications and films. It publishes a bimonthly magazine containing articles on various aspects of hearing, speech, rehabilitation, and related subjects in the field.

There are no other direct patient services, as the association devotes itself to serving member agencies by assisting and upgrading existing programs, as well as initiation of new ones. It is instrumental in recruitment and training programs that include workshops and short courses.

PUBLICATIONS/FILMS
Brochures, charts and monographs are available free of charge in limited quantities. They include the following:

"What a Parent Should Know About Deafness"

"ABC's of Otology"

"Hearing Is Priceless"

Two newsletters are also published by the association. *Hearing and Speech News* is a thirty-two-page magazine which presents articles covering various aspects of hearing, speech, language, rehabilitation, research, and related subjects in the field of human communication. Individual copies may be purchased for 85¢; subscriptions are $5 per year.

Washington Sounds is a monthly newsletter which provides up-to-date coverage of legislation and developments in government agencies which affect the human communications field. Sample copies may be obtained free of charge; subscriptions are $15 per year.

VOCABULARY

Conductive hearing loss —Impairment in hearing caused by interference with conduction of sound through the ear canal and middle ear.

Deaf —A condition of severe to total hearing impairment.

Decibel —A unit of measure for the degree of loudness or intensity of a sound.

Frequency —The specific wave-length of a pure tone.

Hard of hearing —Any degree of hearing impairment that is partial.

Intensity —The degree of loudness of a pure tone expressed in decibels.

Nerve deafness —Hearing impairment resulting from abnormalities affecting the inner ear and/or any of the nerve pathways leading to the brain centers.

Otitis media —Inflammation of the ear drum and related structures in the middle ear.

Dental Problems

Dental caries—another name for tooth decay—is mankind's most prevalent disease. It is estimated that it affects 99 percent of the population. When bacteria form on the surface of the teeth and act upon carbohydrates to produce acids, a gradual breakdown of the enamel and dentine occurs.

Dentists deal with prevention and treatment of decay, *periodontal* diseases, malformations of jaw and facial structure, oral cancer, injuries to the jaw and related structures, and a variety of diseases of the mouth.

Periodontal disease affects the soft tissues (gums), the periodontal fibers which hold the teeth in place, and the bone surrounding the teeth. The most common types of periodontal disease are gingivitis and periodontitis.

The causes of gingivitis are the accumulation of plaque, hard deposits around the neck of the teeth; packing of food between the teeth; and mouth breathing. The condition commonly called pyorrhea usually originates as gingivitis. If the gingivitis is not checked, the inflammation spreads; the gums withdraw from the teeth, forming "pockets" which become filled with bacteria, food residue, and eventually pus.

Malocclusion is the term applied to irregularities in the position of the teeth and the improper coming together of the teeth on closing the jaws. It may be either inherited (such factors as size of jaw and size of teeth are handed down from parents to children) or acquired through harmful habits or early loss of teeth through decay.

Regular dental care begun at an early age is the best preventive measure for malocclusion. The dentist may be able to start procedures which can prevent the need for more complicated treatment at a later date. If special treatment is necessary, the dentist will refer the patient to an *orthodontist*, a dentist especially trained to diagnose and treat malocclusion.

The purpose of orthodontia is not only to improve the appearance of the person. By properly adjusting the placement of the teeth the general efficiency and health of teeth and gums is improved and future trouble caused by misaligned teeth is avoided.

TREATMENT Dental caries occur more frequently in childhood than in maturity. Prevention begins with proper diet, regular brushing of teeth with a fluoride toothpaste, and regular visits to the dentist. Adding fluoride to the water supply has resulted in a significant drop in tooth decay.

In treatment of malocclusion the orthodontist first makes a complete X-ray examination of the mouth, takes measurements, and makes a cast of the teeth and gums. He then places braces on the teeth and the process of redirecting the growth of the teeth begins. After this, the braces are frequently manipulated, moved, and changed by the orthodontist. The entire process sometimes takes several years. Some irregularity of dental occlusion occurs in about ninety-five out of every 100 children in the United States.

MEDICAL PROGRESS The introduction of fluoride to community water supplies can reduce by as much as sixty-five percent the incidence of dental decay in youngsters.

Therapeutic dentifrices which help prevent decay have been developed, as well as mechanical aids (electric toothbrushes, water irrigators) to facilitate oral cleanliness and help prevent decay and gum diseases.

FUTURE GOALS Future goals are the total elimination of decay, the control of gum diseases and their prevention, the development of improved materials for tooth restoration that adhere to tooth surfaces, and better preventive techniques to radically cut down incidence of common oral disease.

TESTS X-rays for detection of caries, periodontal disease, malformations or injuries to jaw and related structures.

SERVICES

SPECIALISTS

Specialists recognized by the American Dental Association work in the fields of: oral pathology, public health dentistry, oral surgery, orthodontics, pedodontics, periodontics, prosthodontics, and endodontics.

The specialties are: *orthodontics*, concerned with the relationship of teeth to bone structure of jaw, including bite and apposition of the teeth; *pedodontics*, the care of the growth, development, and maintenance of the jaw and teeth in children; *periodontics*, limited to care of supporting structure around teeth; *prosthodontics*, concerned with rehabilitation of the mouth by the replacement of missing structures; *endodontics*, newest of the specialties, concerned with inflammations of the pulp of a tooth.

COMMUNITY HEALTH INFORMATION

Local and state dental societies will make referrals to dentists and specialists in the community. They will not recommend a particular dentist but will give the names of several who are listed with them.

STATE HEALTH PROGRAM

State dental programs vary. Local Departments of Health give information about them. The Dental Health Division of the State Department of Health can give specific information on state programs in public dental health. Some states provide all essential dental services, including treatment of malocclusion and dentofacial deformity correction, without charge, to those financially eligible.

FEDERAL RESEARCH PROGRAMS

The National Institute of Dental Research, Bethesda, Maryland, has appropriations of thirty million dollars a year for grants and direct operations. In addition to research into causes, prevention, diagnosis, and treatment of oral and dental diseases and conditions, the Institute provides unique training opportunities; sponsors numerous seminars; and maintains an important interchange of information among various scientific disciplines engaged in dental research.

See page 202 for a description of recent research.

PROFESSIONAL   American Dental Association, 211 East Chicago
ASSOCIATION   Avenue, Chicago, Illinois, 60611. This is a professional service organization with informational
and referral services for the public.

State Dental Associations in every state, including District of Columbia, Panama Canal Zone,
Puerto Rico, and the Virgin Islands. In addition,
there are 450 local societies.

HISTORY OF ASSOCIATION
Founded in 1859 in Niagara Falls, New York,
"to encourage the improvement of the health
of the public and promote the art and science
of dentistry."

SERVICES OF NATIONAL HEADQUARTERS
Referral agency for names of dentists, societies,
and inquiries.

SERVICES OF LOCAL CHAPTERS
All state and local societies offer some referral
service. Some have emergency treatment centers
and several have grievance committees. All provide information and publications. Some operate
clinics and mobile units, in conjunction with state
Boards of Health and other agencies.

The Association offers its services to dental
societies rather than to the general public. Their
councils within the Association are policy-making
agencies which work for improved dentistry.

PUBLICATIONS/FILMS
Some general and specific informational material
on dental health and diseases is available. Films,
slides, and radio transcriptions are available for
various age and interest groups.

VOCABULARY

Dental caries   —A localized, progressive, molecular disintegra-
tion of the teeth, beginning with the dissolution
of the enamel.

Dentine —The substance underlying the enamel over the crown of the tooth. Dentine is related to bone but differs from it in the absence of included cells.

Enamel —The vitreous substance of the crowns of the teeth.

Fluoridation —The addition of chemical salts, fluorides, to the water supply. Experiments with school children who have received a regular intake of one part per million of fluoride in drinking water have established that there is a significant reduction in dental decay when water is fluorinated.

Gingiva —That part of the gum which surrounds the tooth and lies incisal to the crest of the alveolar ridge.

Gingivitis —Inflammation of the gums.

Pericementum —The connective tissue membrane covering the cement layer of a tooth.

Periodontitis —Inflammation of the pericementum.

Diabetes

If researchers in the complex field of metabolic disorders agree on anything at the present time, it is that diabetes is an exceedingly complicated condition about which much remains to be learned. At one time, diabetes was thought to be simply a disorder in which the pancreas failed to produce an adequate supply of *insulin*, a hormone made by the pancreas, whose principal function is to help the body use glucose. This attitude changed radically in the early 1960s, when a technique was perfected for accurately measuring the amount of insulin in the blood. It was found that many diabetics, especially those with mild conditions, have substantial levels of insulin present in the blood along with increased amounts of sugar. This suggests that the insulin made by the pancreas of diabetic individuals may be less effective than the insulin of normal people in removing sugar from the blood and transferring it into the cells where it becomes a source of energy.

The basic cause of diabetes is still unknown. It may develop because the body loses its ability to burn sugar. Most researchers feel that in diabetes the normal secretion of insulin is impaired, or else the insulin itself is ineffective. The presence of antagonists in the blood may also block the action of normal insulin.

Juvenile diabetes begins before fifteen years of age and constitutes only five to eight percent of all diabetes. Diabetes is almost always severe in children; onset is rapid, with progression to severe ketoacidosis and coma in a matter of hours or days. Usually within three months following insulin therapy there is a temporary remission of the diabetic state. Untreated diabetes in young persons strikes with greater force than in older sufferers of the disease.

Common symptoms of diabetes are extreme thirst, frequent urination, constant hunger, loss of weight, itching, easy tiring, changes in vision, and slow healing of cuts and scratches. However, diabetes may be present without any obvious symptoms at all.

TREATMENT In treating diabetics, the doctor and the patient are mainly interested in diet, insulin, and exercise. The diabetic eats a nourishing diet but does not eat an excessive amount of any type of food; he eats limited amounts of the type of food his body no longer handles normally—carbohydrates. If necessary, he takes insulin to add to his own supply. The amount of exercise a patient takes is a factor in determining both his diet and his insulin dosage.

Up to now, all efforts to develop a form of insulin that could be taken by mouth have failed because the digestive juices apparently destroy the hormone. The oral compounds which came into use in 1957 are not insulins nor are they substitutes for insulin, because their action is quite different. It is believed that they lower the blood sugar level by stimulating the production of insulin by the pancreas or by aiding the body to utilize glucose. Unlike insulin, the oral compounds are effective only in certain types of diabetes, mainly mild diabetes in people who develop the disease after they have passed the age of forty.

PROGNOSIS The earlier diabetes is discovered, the easier it is to control. Once discovered, diabetes can be controlled by diet, exercise, and, when necessary, insulin or one of the oral compounds that reduce blood sugar. Neglect of diabetes may lead to an increased risk of coronary disease, cerebral hemorrhage, kidney disease, gangrene, diabetic coma, or death.

MEDICAL PROGRESS In 1921, two Canadians, Dr. Frederick G. Banting and Charles H. Best, a post-graduate student, performed experiments on dogs dying of diabetes —brought on by removal of the pancreas. The affected dogs survived when an extract obtained from the pancreas of a normal dog was injected into the bloodstream. The following year insulin was given for the first time to a diabetic patient, and, wherever indicated, it is used today.

Because regular insulin acts so fast, a single daily dose usually isn't enough to keep sugar levels normal throughout the day; in the first years that this treatment was used severe diabetics took as many as four injections in twenty-four hours. In 1936 slow-acting insulins were developed by compounds of insulin and other materials. It is now possible to synthetically produce in the laboratory an insulin which is chemically identical to natural human insulin; this synthetic insulin, however, is not yet produced commercially.

In England, a team headed by Dr. Dorothy C. Hodgkin of Oxford University succeeded in mapping the configuration of the large, complex insulin molecule. It is hoped that this discovery may lead to the development of theories on how insulin works, which can then be tested in the laboratory.

FUTURE MEDICAL GOALS
Some of the questions to be answered in the future are: Is there a connection between heredity and the thickness of the basement membrane (on the exterior wall of capillaries)? In the early 1960s, it was discovered that in diabetics the exterior wall of the capillary is substantially thicker than it is in nondiabetics. Is there a genetic "market" for diabetes, some physical or chemical sign that will indicate an inherited tendency to diabetes before the disorder becomes overt?

TESTS
Blood glucose tests (often called blood sugar tests) not only pinpoint diabetes in its early stages, but often detect a susceptibility to the disorder. Laboratory tests carried out during routine medical examinations frequently uncover many "hidden" cases—mild diabetes where symptoms arise so gradually they are not always noticed. A diagnosis of diabetes, especially in its early stages, however, depends greatly upon the type of test used and the time of day the test is made.

SERVICES

SPECIALISTS
An *internist*—a specialist concerned with the endocrine glands, the heart, the digestive tract, and the metabolic processes—is particularly qualified to treat diabetes. A *metabolic specialist*, whose concern is the inborn errors of metabolism, also treats diabetes and other related diseases. Most diabetic children are under the care of pediatricians, as well as specialists.

COMMUNITY HEALTH INFORMATION
The American Diabetes Association has fifty affiliates. Information on interesting diets for the diabetic child can be obtained from staff nutritionists at the local Department of Health.

STATE HEALTH SERVICES
Diagnosis and treatment for diabetic children varies from state to state. See pages 192–196 for a list of agencies administering services for the handicapped.

FEDERAL RESEARCH PROGRAM
National Institute of Arthritis and Metabolic Diseases has as its mission to conduct, foster, and coordinate research in treatment of various arthritic, rheumatic, and collagen diseases and in the broad spectrum of metabolic diseases, such as diabetes.

A large-scale study of the natural history of diabetes, the development, incidence, and severity of late diabetic complications, are being conducted as part of a special program of the National Institute of Arthritis and Metabolic Diseases. See page 201.

VOLUNTARY HEALTH ASSOCIATION
American Diabetes Association
18 East 48th Street
New York, N.Y. 10017

The Association is a national organization with fifty-three affiliates.

HISTORY OF ASSOCIATION
The American Diabetes Association was founded in 1940 as a professional society of physicians and other scientists concerned with *diabetes*

mellitus and related problems. In 1964, aware of the rapidly growing prevalence of diabetes, the Association began to reorganize as a national voluntary health association in order to involve the laity and meet more effectively the needs of the diabetic, including the increased support of research.

SERVICES OF NATIONAL HEADQUARTERS
National headquarters is concerned with maintaining and expanding its five basic programs in patient education, professional education, public education, and detection and research. They will make referrals to affiliates and answer questions.

SERVICES OF LOCAL AFFILIATES
Many affiliates make referrals to medical and community resources. Local groups sponsor forty summer camps in twenty-six states for diabetic children, maintaining medical standards suggested by the Association.

PUBLICATIONS/FILMS
In addition to professional literature, the ADA *Forecast* is a pocket-size magazine that reports medical developments; explains various aspects of diabetes; and presents articles for patients and by patients. Published every two months, subscriptions at $3 a year can be ordered from the American Diabetes Association. The ADA also publishes a cookbook and reprints of articles. "Learning About Diabetes," a programmed course of instruction, is a recent, helpful addition.

VOCABULARY

Carbohydrate —An organic substance that belongs to the class of compounds represented by the sugars, dextrins, starches, and celluloses.

Hyperglycemia —An excess of sugar in the blood.

Hypoglycemia —The condition brought about by a low level of glucose in the blood; due to excessive utiliza-

tion of sugar or to interference with the formation of sugar in the liver or to overdose of insulin.

Insulin —The antidiabetic hormone arising from the
islets of Langerhans of the pancreas. In normal
animals or in man, insulin causes a reduction in
blood-sugar.

Ketoacidosis —An increase in the acidity of the blood; a severe
complication that frequently is found in juvenile
diabetes, it often leads to coma and requires
hospitalization.

Drug Addiction

DESCRIPTION OF
CONDITION
Recently a rehabilitation center in New York had a nine-year-old addict in residence. He came to the center the day after his best friend, also nine years old, died of an overdose. The press coverage brought out the fact that not only were there increasingly large numbers of younger addicts, but that there were no rehabilitation facilities legally permitted to treat them. More than half of the addicts in the United States are under thirty years of age.

Drug addiction first became a problem in the United States during the Civil War when wounded men were given injections of morphine to relieve their pain. So many soldiers became addicted that it was called "the army disease."

Before the Harrison Narcotic Act in 1914 there were no effective controls over the use of narcotics in the United States. Through the nineteenth century and up until 1914 a large number of patent medicines with narcotics were advertised and could be bought openly and cheaply.

The term narcotics generally refers to opium and pain-killing drugs made from opium, such as morphine and codeine. These and other opiates are obtained from the juice of the poppy fruit. Heroin, the narcotic used by most addicts today, is made by acetylation of morphine.

When the abuser of a narcotic becomes addicted his body requires repeated and larger doses of the drug. Once the habit starts, larger and larger doses are required to produce the same effects. This occurs because the body develops a "tolerance" for the drug.

When the addict stops using the drug, he suffers withdrawal sickness. The symptoms are severe and painful—sharp abdominal and leg cramps, profuse sweating, chills and shakes. Along with the physical dependence on drugs, the addict develops a psychological dependence. He comes to depend on the drug as a way to escape facing life.

Barbiturates are also addictive and are being used in greater quantities by more and more people. The person addicted to barbiturates will suffer severe irritability and insomnia, possibly accompanied by convulsions, seven to ten days after withdrawal.

According to both state and federal laws, barbiturates are not to be sold without a doctor's prescription and such a prescription cannot be legally refilled without specific orders from a doctor. Unfortunately these laws are violated and there is widespread misuse of these drugs.

TREATMENT Medical authorities say that an addict is a sick person who needs treatment for his physical addiction and withdrawal sickness, and, later, he needs help to keep him from going back to drugs after his withdrawal. Because drug-taking may have become a way of life, this becomes the most difficult part of the treatment.

Addicts who have stayed off drugs for a number of years report that close supervision and continued treatment were the main factors in their rehabilitation.

Many addicts undergo maintenance treatment in community clinics. Some of these clinics dispense methadone and cyclazocine, drugs that block the "high" the addict experiences from heroin.

Others enroll in self-help programs run by ex-addicts. The treatment consists of frank and open group discussions several times a week among the residents, often with the guidance of a professional staff member. Privileges are earned only by hard work.

As drug addiction reaches epidemic proportions, more and more rehabilitation programs are desperately needed, particularly for adolescent and younger addicts.

SERVICES

SPECIALISTS In addition to professionally trained personnel— for example, physicians, psychiatrists, and psychologists—the addict may be helped by former or fellow addicts. Synanon, a pioneer in establishing a treatment center which has no professional staff and in which the residents themselves constitute the therapeutic personnel, has been the model for a number of treatment centers.

COMMUNITY HEALTH INFORMATION
Mental Health Associations (listed on pages 140–146) are a source of treatment facilities. Social service departments of community hospitals can furnish information about programs in those hospitals as well as in others. Many communities have started telephone "hot lines" manned by volunteers and ex-addicts to answer questions and make referrals; some offer emergency services.

National Clearinghouse for Drug Abuse
Information (NIMH)
5600 Fishers Lane
Rockville, Maryland 20852
Phone: (301) 443-4493

This organization has literature and can answer questions about drug abuse; they are not, however, an emergency referral source.

FEDERAL RESEARCH PROGRAM
The Division of Narcotics Addiction and Drug Abuse is responsible for research into the many aspects of drug abuse, including the effects of narcotics, marijuana, LSD, barbiturates and amphetamines.

VOLUNTARY HEALTH ASSOCIATION
American Social Health Association
1740 Broadway
New York, N.Y. 10019

The Association does not have state or local affiliates.

SERVICES OF ASSOCIATION
The American Social Health Association was the first national, voluntary social welfare agency to set up a program in national addiction, giving to this serious and costly problem the attention it warrants. The Association has established a *professional* information center where data on the many facets of addiction are collected; and

it also has literature for the public which deals with the problems of drug abuse and the results of research.

VOCABULARY

Abstinence symptoms — When a drug of the opium group is withheld from an addict, the discomfort is described as abstinence symptoms or withdrawal illness.

Addiction — A state of periodic or chronic intoxication produced by repeated consumption of a drug; occurs when profound changes take place in the chemistry and physiology of the body.

Drug dependence — A state arising from repeated administration of a drug on a periodic or continuous basis. There are usually physical and psychological aspects to a person's dependence.

Habituation — The World Health Organization defines habituation as a condition resulting from the repeated administration of a drug. Its characteristics include: a desire (but not compulsion) to continue taking the drug for the sense of improved well-being that it engenders; little or no tendency to increase the dose; some degree of psychic dependence on the effect of the drug, but absence of physical dependence and, therefore, no abstinence syndrome.

Toxic effects — Poisoning; any substance used excessively can act as a poison or toxin. With drugs, the margin between beneficial dosage and one that produces undesirable effects varies greatly.

Epilepsy

The word epilepsy is derived from the Greek word meaning "seizure." Epilepsy is among the oldest ailments known to man. References to it appear in earliest recorded history even though it still is one of the world's least understood maladies. Some famous persons thought to have suffered from epilepsy were Napoleon, Buddha, Socrates, Alfred Nobel, and Tchaikovsky.

Rather than being classified as a disease, epilepsy is the symptom of a neurological disorder which manifests itself in seizures, resulting from too much energy being discharged from one or more cells of the brain.

Seizures may occur at any age and to any race, sex, family, or individual. A seizure may be very apparent or pass unnoticed by others. Although the common feature of the seizure is a sudden abnormal function of *neurons*, or nerve cells, the seizures differ greatly in terms of how they are experienced by the individual or seen by an observer.

There are various types of seizures: *grand mal, petit mal, infantile myoclonic* and *akinetic, psychomotor, focal motor*, and *febrile*. More than one type of seizure may occur in individuals whose seizures, such as *grand mal, petit mal*, or myoclonic, arise from the nerve cells in the midline brain structure. Similarly, psychomotor and focal seizures may occur in the same patient.

A *grand mal* seizure is a generalized convulsion consisting of loss of consciousness, stiffening, muscle movements, and jerks of the limbs or trunk. Irregular noisy respiration or drooling may occur; and a blue or pale color may be apparent in the face, fingernails, or lips. After such convulsions, sleeping, drowsiness, confusion, or fatigue may be experienced.

Petit mal seizures may occur up to 100 times a day, and generally appear to be merely a blank stare or rapid blinking of eyes, sometimes accompanied by small, twitching movements. These

convulsions, usually occurring in children between six to fourteen, may also affect adults and
are distinguished by the fact that the individual's
activity continues as if nothing had happened
after such a seizure.

Infantile myoclonic and *akinetic* convulsions
are sometimes called "lightning seizures" because of the suddenness and short duration of the
seizure. *Focal cortical* seizures usually arise from
that part of the brain that regulates motor and
sensory function. *Limbic* or *temporal* convulsions
result from lesions in the temporal lobe of the
brain which result primarily in disturbances in
thinking and behavior. *Psychomotor* seizure, the
most complex pattern of behavior, is sometimes
characterized by chewing and lip smacking,
staring and confusion, abdominal aches and head-
aches, and inability to remember what has happened. They may last from one minute to several
hours.

TREATMENT A physician's task is to attempt to find the cause
of the convulsions rather than to merely treat
the patient's symptoms, in order to determine
what specific treatment is needed. A thorough
history, including the time of seizures, factors
such as the presence of fever or infection, the
pattern of the seizures, and awareness of unusual
behavior preceding seizures are essential to a
proper diagnosis.

A complete physical and neurological examination follows the history of the events preceding
the seizure. An electroencephalogram (EEG)—
a written record of electrical current generated
in the brain—will be made. X-rays of the skull
and a spinal tap in the lumbar region are among
other tests often given. Anticonvulsant drugs are
selected on the basis of effectiveness for a particular type of seizure.

PROGNOSIS Modern medical techniques make it possible to
diagnose and treat epilepsy better than ever
before. Discovery and use of anticonvulsants
represented a major breakthrough in the treatment and control of the disorder. The medical

prognosis is bright for approximately eighty percent of patients who could, if properly diagnosed and treated, achieve substantial seizure control with the drugs now available.

Statistics show, however, about twenty percent of epilepsy patients do not respond to treatment with currently available drugs. Though research continues, few significant new drugs have been developed since the discovery of Dilantin. ® For this twenty percent the present outlook is not bright, but a major breakthrough could come at any time.

Even today, many potentially controllable cases go undiagnosed and untreated. This is due to the fact that parents and teachers do not always recognize the symptoms, particularly in the case of *petit mal* (which is often mistaken for day-dreaming) or because they are ashamed to seek medical advice due to the stigma often attached to this disorder.

FUTURE GOALS The major and primary efforts are directed toward total seizure control. It is to be hoped that someday medical science may be able to find a cure and perhaps even prevent epilepsy. An effort is being made to fully control seizures for all types of patients, without the often unpleasant side effects of anticonvulsant therapy.

Scientists are attempting to find the answer to the following questions:

1. What starts an epileptic seizure?
2. What happens chemically in the brain cells during a seizure?
3. What enables a seizure to spread, as it sometimes does, until it involves the entire brain?
4. How do anticonvulsant drugs work, and with what effect on the brain?
5. Is it possible to develop a drug which will prevent seizures in all patients?
6. Why are available drugs ineffective in a number of cases with seizures?

Only when the answers to these questions are known will the medical mystery of epilepsy be solved.

DRUG THERAPY As more individuals with convulsive disorders are recognized and treated, more is learned about the management of different patients and the use of numerous anticonvulsant drugs. However, it is still difficult to predict what drugs will work most effectively and how a given individual with a particular type of convulsive disorder may attain complete control for any period of time. The selection of drugs and administration, therefore, is based entirely on the individual's particular needs. The physician looks for the drug, or combination of drugs, to control convulsions with a minimum of side effects. He initially selects a drug and administers it under careful supervision depending on the reaction of the individual.

The use of several drugs may be necessary to control convulsions, and this requires careful monitoring by clinical examination as well as studies of blood and urine. Although there is no cure for epilepsy, drugs can completely control or substantially reduce the frequency of seizure in the great majority of patients. Some patients have been known to experience remission of seizures as a result of anticonvulsant therapy.

TESTS The electroencephalogram (EEG) or "brain-wave test" is a written record of the brain's electrical activity, and is an important part of the total examination to determine whether or not an individual has epilepsy. In addition, the test may help in the selection of applicable treatment, and furnish information as to the prognosis.

Children are usually fascinated by the EEG equipment and are cooperative. In order to achieve the proper degree of relaxation for the test the doctor may suggest keeping the child up late the night before the test, or give sedatives prior to the examination and play games with him. The recording procedure usually takes between thirty to forty-five minutes.

SERVICES

SPECIALISTS The majority of epileptic patients receive at least initial treatment from a general practitioner or pediatrician. Many are referred to a neurologist, who, because of his precise anatomical knowledge of the nervous system and its function, can determine the exact nature of the disorder and the most appropriate therapy with greater accuracy than a nonspecialist. One of the newest specialists equipped to treat epilepsy is an *epileptologist*, who confines his practice exclusively to this disorder. Psychologists and psychiatrists are helpful to the patient and his family in coping with the psychological problems of this particular handicap.

COMMUNITY HEALTH INFORMATION

The Epilepsy Foundation of America has approximately 104 chapters with additional chapters forming. The Foundation is the only national health organization concerned with epilepsy, but there are about fifteen independent local voluntary organizations. Write the Foundation for the name and address of the chapter nearest you.

HOSPITAL SERVICES

Out of approximately 8,800 hospitals in the United States, fewer than 500 have facilities specifically designed for convulsive disorders. The Epilepsy Foundation makes referrals to these facilities.

STATE HEALTH SERVICES

The Crippled Children's Program in each state has facilities for the diagnosis and treatment of epilepsy and will also make referrals.

FEDERAL RESEARCH PROGRAMS

The National Institute of Neurological Diseases and Stroke (NINDS), the research arm of the National Institutes of Health, Bethesda, Maryland, is concerned with the investigation of the medical mysteries of epilepsy. See page 203 for the scope of their research.

VOLUNTARY HEALTH ASSOCIATION

Epilepsy Foundation of America
1828 "L" Street, N.W.
Suite 406
Washington, D.C. 20036
   The Foundation has 104 chapters.

HISTORY OF ASSOCIATION
In 1967 two national organizations, the Epilepsy Association of America and the Epilepsy Foundation, merged to create a strong and united national voluntary agency that would work effectively on behalf of the nation's more than four million epileptics. The merger brought together an outstanding team of neurologists, epileptologists, psychologists, educators, and others concerned with the problem.

SERVICES OF NATIONAL HEADQUARTERS
The Foundation is the only national voluntary health agency concerned with epilepsy. Together with its network of chapters, the Foundation conducts programs in the areas of research, employment, public information, and patient services.

The National Children's Rehabilitation Center, P.O. Box 360, Leesburg, Virginia, 22075, is an independent organization supported largely by the Epilepsy Foundation of America. Any epileptic child whose intelligence falls within the average range but who suffers from learning, social, or emotional problems is eligible for residence at the Center, as long as he is a resident of the United States or its possessions and is between the ages of six and sixteen.

Consideration is given to whether the student can benefit sufficiently from the Center's programs to be able to return home within a reasonable period. The Center is not designed to provide services for children needing complete individual care, nor for children requiring long-term custodial care.

SERVICES OF LOCAL AFFILIATES
The services provided on the local level range from patient referral to diagnostic evaluation and vocational rehabilitation. Services available through the chapters may vary greatly from area to area. Write to the Foundation's national headquarters for name and address of the nearest chapter.

PUBLICATIONS

The Epilepsy Foundation offers a number of free pamphlets and other information relating to various aspects of epilepsy. Pamphlets are available in reasonable quantities, without charge, to professional groups and students. They include:

"Current Information"
"Teacher's Role"
"Teacher's Tips"
"You, Your Child, and Epilepsy"
"Questions and Answers" (available also in Spanish)
"Don't Be Afraid of the Child with Epilepsy"
"Data-Pak"
"Recognition, Onset, Diagnosis, and Therapy"
"A Patient's Guide to EEG"
"Employer's Role"
"School Alert"

FILMS

A free film-loan service for professional groups and school systems supplements the pamphlets. The Foundation will provide descriptions of the films available, as well as instructions for scheduling.

EDUCATIONAL PROGRAMS

Most children who have epilepsy belong in regular school classes. Today, with more effective seizure control, more and more teachers and school administrators are encouraging and welcoming the epileptic child. The Epilepsy Foundation of America's "School Alert" program is designed to assist teachers, students, parents, and the entire school community with information about epileptic seizures and how to handle them when they occur.

Unfortunately, children with epilepsy are barred from some schools and universities. There are also not enough schools for children who are retarded in addition to being epileptic.

For a description of the National Children's Rehabilitation Center which can accommodate a limited number of children with average intelligence who can benefit from their unique programs, see page 98.

RECREATION Local chapters of the Epilepsy Foundation of America and the National Headquarters have information on summer camps that welcome children with epilepsy. Girl Scouts, Boy Scouts, 4-H, and Camp Fire Girls have special troops for children with a handicap.
NOTE: National Epilepsy League, 2222 North Michigan Avenue, Chicago, Illinois, 60611, offers a discount on medications. Prescriptions may be sent to them for an estimate of cost. Membership in the league is $1.00

VOCABULARY

Aura —A short warning period experienced by some patients just prior to a seizure. Some describe it as a "strange feeling," others say it is an odd odor or a feeling of dizziness. Whatever form the aura takes in any particular patient, it acts as a warning that a seizure is about to occur.

Idiopathic seizures —Seizures for which the principle cause of the convulsions is not known, for example, when there is no demonstrable lesion. The seizure pattern is usually not localized in any part of the brain and the result of a neurological examination proves normal. The electroencephalogram (EEG) pattern, however, shows an altered brain wave pattern.

Postictal state —A period of confusion, general fatigue, and headache, which follows the seizure, usually *grand mal.*

Spike and wave pattern —Brain wave pattern recorded by an electroencephalogram (EEG). Each type of epilepsy has a characteristic pattern.

Status epilepticus —The rapid, repeated recurrence of any type of seizure without recovery between attacks.

Usually applies to *grand mal*-type seizure; the patient is unconscious until given emergency medical treatment.

Symptomatic seizures —Seizures resulting from a known cause such as head injury or birth trauma.

Heart Disease

DESCRIPTION OF CONDITION

Congenital (inborn) heart defects and rheumatic fever are the two disorders responsible for the majority of heart disease in children and young adults.

About 25,000 children are born in this country every year with congenital heart defects. Such defects result from failure of the infant's heart—or of a major blood vessel near the heart—to develop normally before birth. The causes of most of these malformations are still unknown. In some children the defect is so slight that it causes no difficulty. In others it may impair circulation or growth.

A condition sometimes accompanying congenital heart defects is cyanosis. In cyanosis some of the blood which is meant to go first to the lungs for oxygen is pumped directly from the heart to the body. Since blood low in oxygen is bluish-red, it gives the skin a blue tinge (thus, the term "blue babies"). This condition may also appear in childhood or adolescence and can be corrected by surgery.

Rheumatic fever does not necessarily affect the heart, but it is one of the most frequent causes of heart trouble in children. Rheumatic fever may weaken the pumping action of the heart, which may become enlarged. When the inflammation clears up, however, there may be no permanent damage to the child's heart, or so little that he can lead a normal life.

Permanent damage to the heart is usually the result of the inflammation of either or both of the valves on the left side. As the inflammation subsides, the affected valve heals with a scar, which prevents the valve from opening or closing properly and interferes with normal blood flow. This condition is called *rheumatic heart disease*.

Heart murmurs are unusual sounds produced by circulation of the blood through the valves and chambers of the heart. Murmurs which are harmless occur in more than half of all preschool age children. The condition may disappear in adolescence. Some murmurs are an indication of a heart ailment and require a definite medical diagnosis.

TREATMENT   The family physican can usually tell if a child has a congenital abnormality of the heart. He may refer him to a specialist or to a heart center where specialists can determine the exact kind of heart defect and decide whether an operation is advisable.

Over the past twenty-five years many operations have been developed to bring about complete or partial cure of defects of the heart and of the major blood vessels near the heart.

To remedy certain defects inside the heart, a surgeon may use a closed heart procedure, reaching the malformation through a tiny incision in the heart and making repairs by a sense of touch rather than direct vision.

Open heart surgery, aided by the heart-lung machine, is used when there is a defect or group of defects for which the surgeon requires an unobstructed view of the inside of the heart and a long time (from ten minutes to several hours) during which to make repairs.

Heart transplants, which have received tremendous press coverage, open a new era in medicine, with hope for many defects once beyond help.

In 1944, the famous blue baby operation was devised to compensate for the condition caused by a combination of defects resulting in poor oxygenation of the blood. By connecting a branch of the aorta with the pulmonary artery, the operation provides a channel through which more of the blood can be shunted into the lungs to be oxygenated.

No "miracle drug" has as yet been found to cure rheumatic fever. However, once a strep infection is diagnosed, penicillin or other antibiotics will be prescribed to control the infection before it can set off the rheumatic process.

Long-term use of penicillin or sulfa drugs is recommended in patients with a history of rheumatic fever or rheumatic heart disease to protect against strep infections that may cause future attacks. This drug prophylaxis has had good results.

PROGNOSIS Because of major advances in heart surgery in recent years, it is now possible to correct partially or completely most congenital heart defects. However, not every child with a defective heart needs or can benefit from an operation and some malformations are still inoperable.

Perhaps the most encouraging aspect of modern methods and treatment is that even partially corrected heart defects result in considerable improvement in health and energy.

MEDICAL PROGRESS Dramatic advances in surgical techniques and drug prophylaxis have brought health to patients who would otherwise be invalids. Milestones include the blue baby operation, heart-lung machine, and open heart surgery, as well as heart transplant. The latter is still only experimental. Many problems, such as the body's immune response to the heart, have not yet been solved.

FUTURE MEDICAL GOALS It is estimated that in the United States some 350,000 children of school age have rheumatic or congenital heart disease. Prevention of rheumatic fever is a primary goal.

As further advances are made in cardiac surgery, new surgical procedures will undoubtedly be developed for conditions that cannot be corrected at present. The ultimate goal of research in this field is to discover the causes of congenital heart defects and then find ways to prevent them.

DRUG THERAPY Children with a history of rheumatic fever and rheumatic heart disease are prone to repeated attacks, and with each recurrence there is the possibility of permanent heart damage.

Physicians do not rely solely on detection and treatment of strep infections; they prescribe long-term programs to prevent infections through daily use of sulfonamides, or monthly injections of long-acting penicillin, over a period of years.

Some communities provide low-cost or free medication for rheumatic fever prevention. Such programs are designed primarily to remind the family of the importance of long-term medication and to help the patient to remain on it.

Drugs are also used effectively in patients with congenital heart defects to prevent complications, to relieve the symptoms until surgery is performed, or to relieve symptoms throughout the patient's lifetime.

TESTS Congenital heart defects are sometimes diagnosed at birth, or they may be discovered in a routine physical examination during childhood or escape diagnosis until adulthood.

Sometimes a simple but thorough examination by the family doctor will indicate the trouble, although some children do not have symptoms which are obvious. If further examination is necessary, referral will be made to a heart specialist, a *cardiologist*, preferably one who is familiar with heart ailments in the age group of the patient. The cardiologist can determine, through various tests, whether the heart ailment calls for regular check-ups over a long period of time and for special tests, medical care, or surgery. The initial steps taken by the cardiologist usually include history-taking, thorough examination, and one or more of the routine procedures such as X-rays, fluoroscopy, blood tests, and electrocardiography. In some complex conditions, special tests are necessary. These tests can be done only with the safeguards provided by a well-equipped heart center and a well-trained diagnostic team.

In cardiac catheterization, a thin plastic tube *(catheter)* is inserted into an arm or leg vein. The physician watches through a fluoroscope as the tube is slowly advanced through the vein until it reaches the inside of the heart. By taking blood samples, measuring blood pressure and sometimes performing a procedure called *angiocardiography* through the tube, the nature of the defect can be learned. The patient is sometimes anesthetized for this test. In angiocardiography, a special fluid is injected into a blood vessel or into a chamber of the heart. X-ray films of the heart are then taken in succession. As the fluid travels through the great vessels and the individual heart chambers, it helps to show where the malformations are. In this test, general anesthesia is usually given for younger children, but it may not be necessary for older youngsters.

Only a physician, of course, can diagnose rheumatic fever. About half of the streptococcal infections which occur are likely to escape detection because they produce no symptoms. The other half can be suspected by specific clinical signs and symptoms such as fever, headache, abdominal pain, swollen, tender lymph nodes at the angle of the jaw, or a rash. It is often impossible to differentiate streptococcal infections from virus infections with any degree of certainty on clinical grounds alone. Therefore, the physician must seek bacteriological support by taking a throat culture, a simple procedure which involves swabbing the throat.

SERVICES

SPECIALISTS A cardiologist is a specialist in the diagnosis and treatment of disorders of the heart, and *pediatric cardiologists* confine their practice to the treatment of heart disease in children. A *cardiovascular specialist* is concerned with the circulation of blood through the vascular system, and with the functioning of the heart as a pump for the arterial and venous chambers and the blood vessels.

COMMUNITY HEALTH INFORMATION Local Heart Associations can put parents in touch with agencies offering a variety of services. A family physician or the local Department of

Health can make referrals to heart centers or hospitals.

STATE HEALTH SERVICES Two major sources for obtaining medical and surgical care and financial assistance for congenital heart defects are the State Crippled Children's Program and the State Rehabilitation Services Program.

A patient under twenty-one may be referred to the State Crippled Children's agency by the family or clinic doctor, public health nurse, or school or welfare agency. Parents of such patients may also apply to the agency directly. If further diagnostic tests are needed, the agency may arrange to have this done, usually in the child's own state. If surgery is called for, the Crippled Children's agency may arrange for a child to go to a heart center in his home state or nearby.

The agency may assume complete or partial financial responsibility for diagnosis, surgery, hospitalization, and after-care. It may also help to secure transportation if the family cannot provide it.

The Crippled Children's Program and the State Rehabilitation Services Program often work together on a single case. The Crippled Children's agency may provide surgery to a young person up to twenty-one years old. State Rehabilitation Services give guidance in the choice and preparation for a job within the limits of the patient.

FEDERAL RESEARCH PROGRAM The National Heart Institute, created in 1948, was renamed in 1970 the National Heart and Lung Institute with the responsibility of conducting research into the many aspects of heart and chronic lung disease. Appropriations for grants and direct operations of close to $167 million were made by the government (exceeded only by the nearly $186 million appropriated for the National Cancer Institute in 1970). See page 199 for a description of the scope of recent research efforts.

VOLUNTARY
HEALTH
ASSOCIATION

American Heart Association
44 East 23rd Street
New York, N.Y. 10010

The American Heart Association is composed of fifty-five affiliated Heart Associations and their local chapters and divisions in all fifty states, the District of Columbia, New York City, Chicago, Los Angeles, and Puerto Rico.

HISTORY OF ASSOCIATION

The American Heart Association was founded in 1924 as a professional society of cardiologists. In 1948 it was reorganized as a national voluntary health agency, admitting lay people as well as physicians to its governing bodies and directing its efforts toward a program of research, professional and public education, and community services.

SERVICES OF NATIONAL HEADQUARTERS

The national office of the American Heart Association does not operate a direct patient service or referral program. Inquiries and requests received by the national office, however, will be forwarded to the appropriate affiliated Heart Association.

SERVICES OF AFFILIATES

Heart Associations do not give financial aid directly to the family or the individual. Some, however, help to finance heart centers and other community facilities on a demonstration basis. Many aid in maintaining the standards of existing clinics or help develop new or expanded facilities where needed.

Heart Associations, in cooperation with health departments and other agencies, make available low-cost penicillin or sulfa drugs for rheumatic fever patients on long-term therapy.

Because clinics and services vary or change, affiliated Heart Associations should be consulted for information about medical specialists, therapists, home care, and psychiatric services as well as summer recreational activities and facilities for children with cardiac defects. In some instances local associations can furnish information on loan services for sick-room and other rental equipment.

PUBLICATIONS
Single copies of the following publications are available from local Heart Associations.

"Protect Your Child's Heart" (English and Spanish)

"You, Your Child, and Rheumatic Fever"

"Children with Heart Disease: A Guide for Teachers"

"Innocent Heart Murmurs in Children"

"If Your Child Has a Congenital Heart Defect"

Single copies of professional literature are available without charge, for the most part.

FILMS
Two catalogues, "Professional and Public Education Films" and "Publications and Visual Aids for Physicians," list films and professional information available from local Heart Associations.

EDUCATION In some areas the Board of Education provides teachers for children who are confined to their homes, as well as special classes for those with restrictions.

Too often children who have recovered from rheumatic fever are labeled as "heart patients" when no evident heart damage has occurred. Although these children may be on long-term medication, they are not ill and they should take part in the normal school programs. In fact, doctors agree that most children who have had rheumatic fever do not need to have their activities limited. Only in a few severe cases are they placed on restricted activity. When the doctor prescribes full activity it is as important to see that his instructions are carried out as when he prescribes certain limitations.

For the post-operative congenital heart defect patient, home convalescence may range from a few weeks to several months. This period is an important time of adjustment for the child and his family. It is a time when the youngster may need extra reassurance and attention. Until he is well enough to return to school, he may profit from home teaching. Thorough evaluation by the physician will determine whether the youngster should be placed in a class with normal children or in a restricted activity program.

VOCABULARY

Adrenalin —One of the secretions of two small adrenal glands, located just above the kidneys. This secretion, prepared synthetically, is sometimes used to increase the rate of heartbeat, raise blood pressure, and constrict the small blood vessels.

Aorta —The main trunk artery which receives blood from the lower left chamber of the heart.

Aortic stenosis —Narrowing of the large artery that rises from the left chamber of the heart. Aortic stenosis may be the result of scar tissue forming after a rheumatic fever infection.

Arrhythmia —Irregular heartbeat.

Blue babies —Babies having a blueness of skin (cyanosis) caused by insufficient oxygen in the arterial blood; the condition may indicate a heart defect or may be the result of impaired respiration or premature birth.

Open-heart surgery —Surgery performed on the opened heart while the blood stream is diverted through a heart-lung machine; during the operation the machine pumps and oxygenates the blood, replacing the action of the heart.

Hemophilia

DESCRIPTION OF CONDITION Hemophilia, a genetically transmitted disorder of the blood coagulation mechanism, was known in ancient times, and references to the disease are made by the ancient Hebrews in the Talmud and described by the eleventh-century Arabian physician Albacasis. In 1803, an American physician, John C. Otto, accurately described it as a hereditary disease which does not usually affect women, but is transmitted from the mother to her children. Such women, called carriers, do not manifest the symptoms of the disease. But fifty percent of their male offspring, on the average, will have the disease, and fifty percent of their female children will be carriers.

Since Otto's description until recently the disorder was commonly referred to as "bleeder's disease." If a carrier female transmits the abnormal gene to a son he will manifest the bleeding tendency; if it is transmitted to a daughter, she will not manifest any bleeding tendency but could transmit the gene to her offspring. However, there is a high mutation rate that may arise at the time of conception, causing hemophilia in those without prior family history of the disease. This is true of one-third of all hemophiliacs.

The hemophiliac's blood plasma lacks one of several factors necessary for the coagulation of blood. For its victims it has meant internal hemorrhaging with pain, crippling, the necessity of repeated hospitalization for blood transfusion, and infusion of necessary clotting factors. Threat of death from bleeding into the brain, air passages, or other vital organs is constant.

Now, because of a revolutionized method of care made possible by use of clotting factor concentrates isolated from blood plasma, prevention is possible, if quite expensive. With early diagnosis, prompt treatment, and proper management, life-threatening hemorrhages can be a thing of the past.

Problems still stand in the way of a normal life for most hemophilic children because a continuous alert must be maintained for the occurrence of hemorrhages; there is also only a limited supply of clotting factor concentrates and the aforementioned problem of expense. A child with hemophilia requiring complete prophylaxis—constant replacement of clotting factor to prevent bleeding episodes—can cost $12–22,000 a year just for materials. In less severe cases, estimates run from $5,000 to $7,000 a year.

The National Hemophilia Foundation estimates that over 15,000 males in the United States have moderate or severe forms of the disease. An estimated total of 100,000 have the disease in some form.

TREATMENT Comprehensive care clinics provide a total medical program for the hemophiliac. These centers provide an emergency center for control of acute bleeding episodes and a follow-up center where all other problems are cared for.

Treatment of an acute bleeding episode consists of replacement of the missing clotting factor with either fresh frozen plasma, cryoprecipitate or a concentrate.

If there is excessive blood loss, as in gastrointestinal bleeding, the blood loss must be replaced. If a joint or muscle is involved the limb is usually splinted. Pain may be controlled with analgesics, but aspirin or aspirin-containing compounds are very dangerous because they accentuate the clotting problem. Further treatment consists of physiotherapy to maintain the musculature of the extremity and maintain motion at the joint.

PROGNOSIS In the past, recurrent episodes of bleeding into the joints caused deformity of the extremities and painful arthritis. Bleeding into the stomach or intestines was often fatal. With the advent of replacement products for the missing clotting factors, the outlook has become much brighter. Bleeding episodes can be controlled and the prognosis for a near-normal life is possible.

MEDICAL PROGRESS The most significant advance has been the production and use of various concentrated forms of the missing clotting factors. Treatment is now available for control of bleeding episodes. As a result, there has been, for most patients, a dramatic reduction in pain, crippling, hospitalization, and mortality. The ability to perform surgery on the hemophiliac has also been improved and has aided in the correction of deformities.

Another important development is the establishment of hemophilia centers with specially trained professional staffs and the most advanced treatment methods.

FUTURE GOALS The goal is to perfect the prophylactic therapy for the disease. In the near future it may be possible to control bleeding with frequent intravenous injections of the missing factors. Presently, all these factors must be concentrated from blood. Ultimately it is hoped that the factors can be synthesized inexpensively and even be taken by mouth. While the optimistic long-range aim is to eliminate the disease altogether, the reachable goal is preventive therapy rather than treatment of bleeding episodes.

TESTS A patient's history is frequently insufficient to determine the possibility of a coagulation deficiency. The *clotting time*, a rough determination of the blood's ability to clot in a test tube, may be normal even in the presence of the disease. More sophisticated tests can determine a coagulation deficiency, but an assay of the important clotting factors is necessary for an exact determination of the disorder. A determination may also be made to make sure that a circulating anticoagulant or antibody to the missing factor is not present. The anticoagulant or antibody may be present in up to twenty percent of hemophiliacs and renders them resistant to therapy.

More sophisticated tests are being evaluated which may, in a certain number of cases, indicate whether a female is a carrier. Tests are ninety to ninety-five percent accurate.

SERVICES

SPECIALISTS

Between fifteen and twenty specialized hemophilia centers have recently been developed in hospitals in the United States for the care of patients with serious hemorrhages, as well as for surgery and management of the complications of hemophilia. Multidisciplinary teams—including pediatricians, hematologists, clinical pathologists, orthopedic surgeons, psychiatrists, dentists, social workers, physical therapists, and other specialists—provide diagnosis, continuing comprehensive care, and rehabilitation.

Hospitals may stock cryoprecipitate or concentrates for care of acute bleeding episodes.

The National Hemophilia Foundation provides lists of centers and their services.

COMMUNITY
HEALTH
INFORMATION

The National Hemophilia Foundation and their fifty-four regional chapters have information and make referrals to their centers.

FEDERAL RESEARCH
PROGRAM

The National Institute of Arthritis and Metabolic Diseases is concerned with the problems of hemophilia. See page 201 for the scope of their work and recent findings of the hazards of aspirin.

VOLUNTARY
HEALTH
ASSOCIATION

The National Hemophilia Foundation
25 West 39th Stret
New York, N.Y. 10018
There are fifty-four regional chapters.

HISTORY OF ASSOCIATION

The National Hemophilia Foundation was founded in 1948 by Mr. Robert Henry, the father of a child with hemophilia, who believed that a national health agency would have to be created in order to provide the services and facilities needed by hemophiliacs.

Today there are fifty-four chapters in the National Hemophilia Foundation (NHF). The program, national in scope, supports blood banks, treatment centers, and clinics which daily serve the needs of thousands of individuals.

SERVICES OF NATIONAL HEADQUARTERS
The Foundation stimulates and assists chapters in development of social service programs in the community. It issues periodic newsletters and assists in the publication of materials dealing with research findings and further seeks to interest Federal agencies in sponsoring research. It makes referrals to treatment centers and has publications for hemophiliacs and their families and for medical personnel and professional groups.

SERVICES OF LOCAL AFFILIATES
As a result of the Foundation's efforts to improve the care and treatment of children and adults, a network of blood centers has been set up across the country to service thousands of patients in cooperation with blood banks, clinics, and medical institutions.

Chapters have broadened their services to include nonmedical areas, such as education, vocational guidance, rehabilitation, and counseling on social, family, and psychological problems.

PUBLICATIONS/FILMS
The following literature is of interest to hemophiliacs and their families:
"New Perspective on Hemophilia"
"The Hemophiliac and His School"
Two films, "The Threshold" and "Home Infusion," are available.

VOCABULARY

ANTI-hemophilic factor (AHF) — Also called ANTI-hemophilic globulin (AHG) or Factor VIII, this is the clotting factor missing in classic hemophilia, the most common form of the disease.

Concentrates — Any form of commercially prepared and concentrated Factor VIII or Factor IX.

Contracture — Inability to completely straighten out a joint, usually as a result of hemorrhage.

Cryoprecipitate — A blood product with clotting factor isolated by special laboratory technique, frozen and stored.

Fresh-frozen plasma — The frozen preparation of the liquid portion of blood.

Hemophilic arthropathy — The arthritis or joint damage caused by recurrent hemorrhage into the joints.

Kidney Disease

The kidneys are bean-shaped organs located high on the rear wall of the abdominal cavity whose chief function is elimination of waste substances from the blood through the formation of urine.

There are various diseases of the kidneys. Each has different specific causes, affecting different parts of these organs.

A recent study indicates that at least three million Americans have an unrecognized and undiagnosed disease of the kidneys known as *pyelonephritis*. In this disease the infectious inflammation of the kidney tissue, which at the onset may not interfere with kidney function, may lead to gross disturbances if untreated.

Acute nephritis or *glomerulonephritis* is in most instances a disease of young adults and children. Two-thirds of all cases occur in children under seven years of age. In the usual case, the child has had a sore throat or skin infection due to a streptococcal infection, which seemingly has subsided without difficulty. Then, in one to two weeks, there is the onset of loss of energy, pallor, puffiness of the eyelids. After another day or two, there is a sudden onset of dark coffee-colored urine which results from blood cells in the urine.

Recent evidence indicates that intensive and early penicillin treatment of streptococcal infections may prevent the development of acute glomerulonephritis in some instances. However, antibiotics do not affect the course of glomerulonephritis once the disease has developed.

When there is an incomplete recovery, the disease may progress from the acute stage to subacute stage, and may occasionally evolve into *chronic glomerulonephritis*. Chronic glomerulonephritis frequently has no accompanying symptoms, and its presence can be established only by medical examination. There are various defensive measures that may help the patient with the condition—regulating the diet and using antibiotics and other drugs—but there is no known treatment which will eradicate the disease.

The term *nephrosis* and *the nephrotic syndrome* are used by physicians almost interchangeably to describe a condition in which there is a large and abnormal loss of protein in the urine because of kidney damage.

Childhood nephrosis is uncommon; it affects boys about twice as frequently as girls. There is no known cause for it and no way of predicting its emergence. Usually the swelling which accompanies the disease remains, or in some cases fluctuates, for long periods. A problem associated with the swelling is the danger of infection, which at one time was a common cause of death.

Although kidney disease frequently results from injurious agents such as bacteria, it is also very common for the kidneys to be damaged indirectly as a result of diseases which affect the flow of urine out of the kidney and along the urinary tract. These urinary tract obstructive diseases include a host of congenital or acquired abnormalities which block normal urine flow and, thereby, lead to kidney damage and failure.

TREATMENT Prompt treatment of streptococcal infections in the throat or skin may prevent the development of glomerulonephritis. After the disease has developed, however, the patient generally is kept in bed and given a diet low in salt and protein. Careful observation, to detect early signs of complications, and prompt treatment are essential. After several weeks, there is a cessation of evident blood in the urine and the patient improves with return of strength and appetite. At this point, the diet is liberalized and activity is resumed in relation to the patient's stamina and general well-being. Complete recovery generally occurs in less than a year.

Nephrosis may subside rapidly and spontaneously and, in a small percent of patients, permanently. Usually the swelling stays for long periods, with the danger of infection. Steroids can effectively keep the child in nearly normal health with no swelling and normal urine. When such treatment is effective the danger of infection is reduced. However, steroids do not cure the disease. Often after long periods of good health there may be a relapse. Repetition of the steroid treatment is usually effective. However, it is necessary to continue to check the urine frequently for protein for many years (there is a simple test which can be done at home) before one can feel that a complete cure has been achieved.

Acute kidney failure is usually managed conservatively with a low-salt and low-protein diet and drugs to control blood pressure. If these measures are ineffective, two mechanical means of ridding the body of waste materials are available. In *peritoneal dialysis*, the internal lining of the abdominal cavity is used to filter the wastes; in the other method, which employs the well-known "artificial kidney" dialysis, waste is filtered from the blood directly.

Artificial kidney machines often can be secured on a rental or loan basis for home use or for in-hospital treatment. The Kidney Foundation is a good source of information and advice on this method of treatment.

Kidney disease does not necessarily mean kidney failure. In fact, many disease processes which are not extensive do not cause failure of kidney function and allow the patient's kidney to function well enough to support adequate life. Only in cases when *both* kidneys cannot perform adequately may transplantation of one kidney be considered. Over 5,000 such transplants have been performed around the world.

Kidney transplants date back to 1954. Closer tissue matching has increasingly reduced the risk of rejection. If rejection of the kidney occurs, a patient may go back on the artificial kidney to await another transplant.

PROGNOSIS Following the acute phase of glomerulonephritis there is a gradual improvement over three to seven months with eventual complete recovery in ninety-five to ninety-seven percent of the cases.

No specific treatment is available to prevent the transition from acute glomerulonephritis, with its excellent prognosis, to chronic nephritis, with a varying outlook for complications and reduced life-span.

In about eighty percent of all cases childhood nephrosis can be controlled by steroids. Although such treatment does not cure the disease, it can keep the child in nearly normal health. The other twenty percent of the cases constitute a continuing problem to doctors. However, continued research has brought alternative treatments.

TESTS One to two weeks after an infection due to streptococcus has seemingly subsided, a loss of energy, pallor, puffiness of the eyelids and perhaps the feet, followed by a sudden onset of bloody urine may indicate the possibility of kidney disease. Tests of the urine for traces of blood and albumin will indicate the presence of infection.

In patients with chronic nephritis, tests may indicate a gradual development of high blood pressure or renal failure which could ultimately result in severe illness.

In childhood nephrosis, in contrast to the findings in nephritis, the measurement of blood pressure will probably be normal. Also the degree of swelling is likely to be much more marked for nephrosis. When finger pressure is applied to the skin a definite transient dimple will remain.

Blood tests in the nephrotic syndrome will indicate a low concentration of protein and a rise in fatty substances of which cholesterol is the most commonly measured. The concentration of non-protein-nitrogen (NPN) or blood urea nitrogen (BUN) is measured to indicate whether or not the kidneys are getting rid of waste products. In the nephrotic syndrome, particularly early in the disease, these concentrations will probably be normal—another difference from nephritis, where they may be elevated.

SERVICES

SPECIALISTS A pediatrician is trained to care for most child-hood kidney diseases. A *pediatric nephrologist* confines his practice to children with kidney disease and has additional training in this field. Some surgeons specialize in surgery and transplants of kidneys.

COMMUNITY HEALTH INFORMATION The National Kidney Foundation has forty affiliates in thirty-five states who make referrals to hospitals with facilities for the diagnosis and treatment of kidney disease.

STATE HEALTH SERVICES Although services vary from state to state, each state provides diagnosis, medical supervision, hospitalization, and drugs. Some states may not provide surgical procedures but will make arrangements with neighboring states.

FEDERAL RESEARCH PROGRAM National Institute of Arthritis and Metabolic Diseases carries on research in various aspects of urological and renal disease. The Institute conducts a program in transplantation immunology and the improvement of artificial kidneys and related treatment for patients with chronic kidney failure. See page 201 for a description of recent research.

VOLUNTARY HEALTH ASSOCIATION National Kidney Foundation
116 East 27th Street
New York, N.Y. 10010
There are forty affiliates in thirty-five states and the District of Columbia.

HISTORY OF ASSOCIATION
Incorporated in 1950 in New York State as the National Nephrosis Foundation, the name changed to National Kidney Disease Foundation in 1958. The word "Disease" was dropped from its title in 1964. The Foundation is the only voluntary health organization in the country devoted to the problems of kidney disease.

SERVICES OF NATIONAL HEADQUARTERS
National headquarters primarily deals in referrals to affiliates, and the distribution of public and professional educational materials.

SERVICES OF AFFILIATES
Services vary depending upon community resources. Affiliates are a source of information and advice on community facilities. Many communities are currently testing detection programs for the "warning signs" of kidney disease. Other services may be:

Drug Banks: Drugs are made available at reduced prices or at cost.

Artificial Kidneys: Machines often can be secured on a rental or loan basis for home use rather than in-hospital treatment.

Transplantation: The Foundation can supply a partial list of medical surgical teams with some experience in the field of transplantation.

Organ Donor Program: Widespread distribution of a Uniform Donor Card covering the donation of all organs including kidneys after death. This program will ultimately make available a greater supply of donor kidneys.

PUBLICATIONS/FILMS
Literature dealing with various aspects of kidney disease is available from national headquarters and affiliates. Among the titles are:
"Acute Glomerulonephritis"
"Childhood Nephrosis"
"Your Kidneys"
"Kidney Transplantation"
A wide variety of professional literature and films is available.

NOTE: It costs up to $36,000 a year for three treatments a week in profit-making hospitals and kidney centers. Researchers have had success in reducing the costs of artificial kidney therapy by treating the patient in his home rather than in a hospital. Dialysis machines cost from $2,500 to $5,000. Disposable filters and tubing, which are generally used only once, run as high as $14 to $28 per treatment. The cost averages $3,500 a year to treat the patient at home.

VOCABULARY

Acute glomerulonephritis —A noninfectious inflammation involving the glomeruli throughout both kidneys.

Chronic glomerulonephritis —A noninfectious inflammation that may infrequently evolve from acute glomerulonephritis. Most often it persists without symptoms for many years. There is slow but progressive damage to the glomeruli and the inevitable result in uremia.

Diuretic —A drug which increases the flow of urine.

Nephron —Consists of a tuft of tiny blood vessels called a glomerulus and an attached tube, the tubule. Each kidney contains about one million of these functioning units.

Nephrotic syndrome —A noninflammatory disease, involving the glomerular membrane and resulting in the escape of large amounts of protein molecules from the blood into the urine.

Learning Disabilities/Minimal Brain Dysfunction

The National Advisory Committee on Handicapped Children of the Office of Education recently suggested the following definition from the point of view of an educator:

> Children with special learning disabilities exhibit a disorder in one or more of the basic psychological processes involved in understanding or in using spoken or written languages. These may be manifested in disorders of listening, thinking, talking, reading, writing, spelling, or arithmetic. They include conditions which have been referred to as perceptual handicaps, brain injury, minimal brain dysfunction, dyslexia, and development aphasia. They do not include learning problems which are due primarily to visual, hearing, or motor handicaps, to mental retardation, emotional disturbance or to environmental disadvantage.

From the medical point of view, a minimally brain-injured child is a child whose brain might have developed in a normal manner, but was injured before, during, or after birth due to difficult or prolonged labor, anoxia (lack of oxygen), Rh factor, or other causes. The category also includes children who have suffered from a severe childhood illness with sustained or prolonged high fever, encephalitis, meningitis, or other infection, or trauma as a result of a fall or a blow on the head. Any of these injuries can result in damaged or destroyed brain cells to a greater or lesser degree. A child can become brain-injured at any age through accident or illness.

Whatever the terms used to describe the condition—and there are more than forty definitions—the focal condition is a neurological one that may have organic confirmation. Most frequently, however, the defect is so subtle or slight that such confirmation is impossible.

A recent survey indicates that one to three per-cent of the school population have severe impair-ment; five percent have moderate impairment; while twenty percent have mild to slight impair-ment, which, nevertheless, interferes with learning.

Early brain-damage may lead to a wide variety of disturbances, depending on the location, extent, and type of the damage and the age of the individual at the time of the injury. These types of neurological symptoms appear, either singly or in combination: convulsive (epilepsy); motor (cerebral palsy); intellectual; sensory and percep-tual; language; behavioral disturbances.

The characteristics of brain-injured children, therefore, are many and varied. Some can be found to some degree in any normal child at some stage of development. In brain-injured children they may appear in extreme and inappropriate forms. Most children, for example, develop cer-tain behavior problems very early because of continued frustration when they are ignored or ostracized by peers, siblings, and even parents.

Unlike the mentally retarded child whose intel-ligence is limited because the brain apparently did not develop normally from the beginning, or because the brain was severely damaged, many brain-injured children have normal or above nor-mal intelligence. Most have learning problems due to their perceptual, conceptual, and/or behavior difficulties which cause them to func-tion at lowered levels.

Motor impairment (cerebral palsy), recurrent convulsions (epilepsy), and mental subnormality (retardation) are described in separate chapters. Perceptual or conceptual difficulties accompanied by behavior problems will be described in this chapter.

Perceptual Difficulty: Perception is a process of the senses which normally occurs when an ob-ject is seen, a sound is heard, or even when some-thing is touched, tasted, or smelled and there is understanding of the experience. Brain-injured children sometimes have difficulty understanding the relationship of parts to the whole and cannot grasp a scene or situation in its entirety. Since they tend to highlight irrelevant details, they are apt to have a distorted version of the perceived object. For example, on a printed page they may not perceive whole words or sentences. The letters or even the strokes in a single letter may appear to them as separate images.

Distractibility: Distractibility is a major problem of the minimally brain-injured child. In a schoolroom full of bright pictures, toys, and a large number of active children, the brain-injured child may react to every distraction and be unable to concentrate on the subject of the moment.

Perseveration: To persevere is to persistently pursue a course of action until completed and it is usually a highly commendable characteristic. To perseverate is to carry a response beyond the limits necessary or appropriate to a given situation. Perseveration frequently occurs in a brain-injured child when he is experiencing difficulty or anticipating an exciting event. He may then repeat the same action or phrase over and over again, despite the fact that, for example, a drawing has been finished, or a question has been answered satisfactorily.

Hyperactivity: Most children are quite active especially while playing or attending an exciting event, sometimes to the point of being temporarily uncontrollable. However, hyperactivity as found in some brain-injured children is disorganized and purposeless activity.

EDUCATION Throughout the United States educational services for minimally brain-injured children are far less adequate than those for normal children. Only one state, California, specifies within the context of the law the type of program to be given children with learning disabilities. The majority of state programs are regarded as short term or remedial in nature, anticipating a termination point when the children will be absorbed into regular classes. Virtually no special program exists for adolescents.

The general problems in providing a good program are the lack of standardization of definitions of various conditions; small number of special programs geared to meet varied functional abilities; few specially trained teachers; and few universities offering courses in this area.

PROGNOSIS   Educational opportunities for development are essential for the brain-injured. A large percentage of these children can be almost completely rehabilitated through educational training. The brain-injured child with normal intelligence can, with appropriate educational methods and supportive parental involvement, become a literate, productive adult. For other children who are retarded in addition to being brain-injured, the outlook is less encouraging. They will be dependent over a long period of time and require extended educational and vocational training.

TESTS   A physical examination may give clues to the extent of brain-injury damage in some cases. If the brain damage is too slight or superficial, even an expert neurologist will be unable to give confirmed organic findings. Postural and mobility tests, however, will often show significant indications of brain damage. The child may be unable to hold his extended hands still while concentrating on another task; there may be drifting of the hands or spreading of the fingers, which are signs of cerebellar disease. The consistent lowering of one arm or the inability of the child to make the eyes converge on a near object can be indicative of muscle weakness.

The child with brain damage often has an awkward gait: he does not swing his arms in rhythm with his steps as other children do. There are dissociated movements in talking; loss of normal smooth coordination of respiration and speech; absence of appropriate facial expression and gestures. Sometimes there is poor eye coordination or the finger-to-nose test is awkwardly performed. The electroencephalogram usually is normal in the brain-damaged. If it is abnormal it may show the convulsion pattern, or some localizing signs.

Drawings may be used as a test. The normal

child scribbles at two years, draws a circle at three, copies a square at four, a triangle at five or six, and a diamond at seven years. Children with cerebral damage usually have difficulties with angles, with the overlapping of figures, and with horizontal and vertical drawings.

Results of intelligence tests may indicate a wide discrepancy between the verbal I.Q. and performance I.Q. scores. The full score I.Q. may be 100, the verbal score 120 and performance score as low as 70 or 80. A variety of these tests may be used.

SERVICES

SPECIALISTS   There is a critical shortage of teachers trained in specialized education for children with learning disabilities. Pediatricians, neurologists, psychiatrists, ophthalmologists, optometrists, occupational, and physical and speech therapists are the professional staff that may treat brain-injured children.

COMMUNITY HEALTH INFORMATION   Local schools can give information about specialized local programs; the state boards of education have information on programs throughout the state. The Association for Children with Learning Disabilities with its affiliated parent groups also has information about community resources.

STATE PROGRAMS   Programs vary from state to state. Few programs are initiated without parent pressures pointing out the need. California has the largest number of classes for children with learning disabilities. Information is available from the Board of Education; and Association for Children with Learning Disabilities.

Some states provide a tuition subsidy for a child in a private school, if a special program is not provided in the public school system.

VOLUNTARY HEALTH ASSOCIATION   Association for Children with Learning Disabilities (ACLD)
2200 Brownsville Road

Pittsburgh, Pennsylvania 15201
There are thirty-nine state parent-oriented groups. A directory lists all affiliates and other organizations in each state interested in the problem.

SERVICES OF NATIONAL HEADQUARTERS
Refers inquiries to state affiliates; literature.

SERVICES OF LOCAL AFFILIATES
Information about community resources and literature is provided. The activities of these groups are highly varied. Some may stimulate legislation; some run small schools or summer day camps. The New York ACLD affiliate, for instance, operates two demonstration schools, several year-round recreation programs, and services for pre-teens and adolescents.

VOCABULARY

Dyslexia — Impairment of the ability to read.

Hyperkinetic essential — A condition, seen in children, marked by excessive and sustained voluntary and involuntary movements.

Perception — Recognition of an object in response to sensory stimuli; the act or process by which the memory of certain qualities of an object is associated with other qualities impressing the senses, making possible recognition of the object.
    depth perception — The ability to estimate depth or distance between points in the field of vision.
    space perception — The recognition of an area, dimensions, or position occupied, or any space, through the senses.
    stereognostic perception — The recognition of objects by touch.

Mental Illness/Autism

MENTAL ILLNESS

It is estimated that as many as 500,000 children in this country suffer from psychoses, borderline psychoses, and borderline psychotic conditions and that another million are afflicted with personality and character disorders. Of the fifty million school-age youngsters, evidence suggests that between ten and twelve percent have moderate to severe emotional problems requiring some kind of mental health service. The American Medical Association has labeled mental illness the nation's number one health problem.

Mental illness can roughly be divided into two main categories. The first, *psychoses*, refers to very serious mental illness, in which people seem to live in imaginary worlds of their own. Organic psychoses are those stemming from physical causes. Functional psychoses have no known physical causes. Schizophrenia is the most common of all psychoses and affects young people more than any other form of mental illness.

The second category, *neuroses*, while less severe, can cause a person considerable suffering. Some symptoms of neuroses may include the feeling of being unloved, inferior, and inadequate (often without reason), a constant sense of guilt, dread, and fear, chronic tiredness and nervous tension, certain pronounced phobias such as fear of high or closed-in places and other abnormal reactions. Everyone has some of these feelings some of the time, but the neurotic person has them to a greater degree most of the time, often interfering with his life and peace of mind.

Between ten and twenty-two percent of children and youths under eighteen years of age in this country, depending on the criteria for different psychological conditions, have emotional and behavioral difficulties that require assistance. For each psychiatrist, psychologist, social worker, and nurse in mental health programs for children, there are thousands of children with emotional and behavioral difficulties. This makes dramatically clear that mental health professionals have not and cannot meet directly the needs of an overwhelming number of children.

Because of the lack of manpower in the mental health disciplines, a significant number of children receive services from those outside the mental health disciplines, such as nonpsychiatric physicians, social workers, welfare workers, public health nurses, and clergymen.

As help becomes more readily available through community treatment services the chances of recovery from mental illness increase. Services which include various kinds of outpatient care, psychiatric units in general hospitals, and special treatment centers for mentally ill children are important to all communities. Unfortunately many Mental Health Centers seldom treat severely ill children beyond diagnosis. Some institutions set as their criteria for admission that the child be self-feeding, self-dressing, toilet-trained, and verbal, eliminating the severely mentally ill child, such as the autistic or schizophrenic.

MEDICAL PROGRESS One of the most significant medical advances in the treatment of mental illness has been the use of drugs, beginning in 1954 with the development of chlorpromazine. The tranquilizing drugs make it possible to calm patients without stupefying them, and they are then able to respond to other forms of treatment.

In the last ten years another important advancement in the treatment of mental illness has been the trend toward community treatment. Rather than being sent to remote mental hospitals, an increasing number of children can now be offered a variety of treatments in their own communities.

FUTURE MEDICAL GOALS Medical goals in the future will be the continued research into the causes and prevention of mental illness where physical causes can be found. Biochemists and geneticists working in this area in recent years have been coming up with important findings. Expansion of community care centers is also a goal.

DRUG THERAPY

Sedation is used as a temporary device to quiet the patient's anxiety, restlessness, or agitation. The sedative might be anything from a mild barbiturate to a more powerful drug that puts the patient to sleep.

"Tranquilizers," which are also used in treatment, are different from sedatives in that they do not just dull the senses, but actually make symptoms such as anxiety, agitation, and delusions disappear and leave the patient in a generally relaxed, clear-headed, and peaceful frame of mind.

SERVICES

SPECIALISTS

Psychiatrist — A medical doctor who has had additional formal training of three years in psychiatry, with two years' experience in the branch of medicine concerned with diagnosis and treatment of mental illness and mental retardation. A child psychiatrist has additional specialized training.

Psychologist — A nonmedical professional with extensive accredited graduate training in experimental or clinical psychology, who must have a Masters Degree and usually a Ph.D.

Psychoanalyst — Either a medical doctor or a nonmedical professional who confines his practice to the application of formal psychoanalysis.

Neurologist — A medical doctor who confines himself mainly to the inflammatory, degenerative, and neoplastic diseases of the nervous system. Mental diseases and nervousness which we associate with the "mind" are now the concern of the psychiatrist rather than the neurologist.

COMMUNITY HEALTH INFORMATION

Two sources of information and patient service are the Mental Health Association and the State Mental Health Authority. See pages 140–146 for a list of these in each state. The National Society for Autistic Children has an information and referral service for mentally ill children. See page 136.

The Family Service Association of America is another source of direct patient service. There are more than 340 agencies in the United States and Canada that offer counseling in the areas of child and teen-age behavior, planning around physical and mental disorders, parent-child conflicts, etc. Local agencies vary according to community needs and resources. Fees are charged according to the family's ability to pay. The agencies are listed in the local telephone directory. The Mental Health Association can make referrals to religious affiliated agencies that provide services.

STATE MENTAL SERVICES See pages 140–146.

FEDERAL RESEARCH PROGRAM See pages 204–205.

VOLUNTARY HEALTH ASSOCIATION The National Association for Mental Health
1800 North Kent Street
Rosslyn Station
Arlington, Virginia 22209
State Affiliated Divisions have information on local chapters. See pages 140–146.

HISTORY OF ASSOCIATION

Clifford W. Beers' frightful experience in mental hospitals at the beginning of the century led to the formation of what is now the National Association for Mental Health. In February 1909, Beers wrote an autobiographical account of his sufferings as a mentally ill person in his book *A Mind That Found Itself*. The book stimulated interest in the need for radical change in the care of the mentally ill. Beers and the other twelve charter members, among them psychologist William James, felt the time was long overdue for the establishment of a permanent agency for reform and education in the field of mental and nervous disorders.

In 1950 the Mental Health Committee merged

with the more recently formed National Mental Health Foundation and the Psychiatric Foundation to become the National Association for Mental Health.

The Association is made up of volunteer laymen and professionals and has no connection with any government agency. It is supported solely by contributions from individuals, firms, foundations, and in some areas by United Funds.

SERVICES OF NATIONAL HEADQUARTERS

The national office refers individuals to the appropriate division or chapter, rather than providing direct services. It directs a research program, a public information program, and acts as the liaison with governmental and private organizations. Field representatives work closely with divisions and chapters.

SERVICES OF LOCAL AFFILIATES

Some chapters provide direct services in the form of clinics, halfway houses and other facilities. Others make referrals and provide information on clinics, treatment centers, and hospitals.

PUBLICATIONS/FILMS

"Mental Illness—A Guide for the Family"
"The Mentally Ill Child"
"What Every Child Needs for Good Mental Health"

These are pamphlets designed to acquaint the public with the various aspects of mental health. The Association has a catalogue of selected publications and films that may be rented or purchased.

EDUCATION Either the National Association for Mental Health or the State Mental Health Authority makes special referrals to institutions and schools for the mentally ill child.

The National Society for Autistic Children also makes referrals and keeps an up-to-date file of institutions and schools.

VOCABULARY

Catatonia —A symptom that occurs commonly in schizo-phrenia; in passive form, the patient exhibits withdrawn muscular attention, stays motionless, and refuses food. In the active state, which is much rarer, the patient is impulsive and bel-ligerent.

Ego —In Freudian theory, the central part of the personality which deals with reality and is influenced by social forces. The ego serves as moderator between unconscious impulses and personality plus social standards. It is the vehicle through which the personality habitually deals with situations.

Paranoia —Mental disorder characterized by delusions, such as grandeur or persecution.

Psychotherapy —Treatment of mental illness of largely psychological and verbal means (using no drugs or treatment), based on psychoanalytic theory in which a person recognizes his conflict and learns to deal with it. It involves the patient's gaining insight into the unconscious motivation for his behavior, thoughts, and emotional response.

Schizophrenia —The most common of psychoses; involves disorders of thoughts and moods; characterized by a withdrawal from reality with hallucination and delusions.

AUTISM

DESCRIPTION OF CONDITION The autistic child lives completely wrapped up in himself with little contact with reality. He lacks meaningful speech, although he can often repeat with astounding accuracy such things as television commercials.

At times the autistic child seems extremely alone, may sit and play for hours with his fingers or bits of paper—lost in a world of fantasy. At other times, he may be hyperactive, with behavior that is hard to manage. Many autistic children can go for days with little sleep or food. These behavioral patterns make this condition one of the most puzzling of medical mysteries.

There is no known cause for autism. However, research findings point to the possibility of bio-chemical error. Although there is also no known cure, some autistic children benefit, often dra-matically, from special education suited to their needs. Unfortunately few states have developed programs especially for autistic children.

TREATMENT There is yet no treatment in the usual sense of the word. The most successful method of amelio-ration at this time is highly structured education, including reinforcement therapy.

Some parents have reported marked improve-ments after massive doses of specific vitamins. Evidence is accumulating which seems to indicate that an inordinately high percentage of autistic children have hypoglycemia and/or celiac dis-ease. When these conditions are treated, behav-ior improves.

PROGNOSIS It is the experience of parents and knowledgeable professionals that the earlier and longer a child receives a good educational experience, the more likely he is to "make it"—that is, stay out of a mental institution. But in very few known cases have autistic children later achieved a near-normal adulthood.

SERVICES

SPECIALISTS Teachers, audiologists, speech therapists, pedia-tricians, psychiatrists, and biochemists all work to treat and solve the mysteries of autism.

COMMUNITY HEALTH INFORMATION The National Society for Autistic Children has seventy local chapters. Write National Head-quarters, 621 Central Avenue, Albany, New York, 12206, for locations.

STATE HEALTH SERVICES Nonexistent for the most part. Some autistic children are admitted to Child Guidance Clinics.

VOLUNTARY HEALTH ASSOCIATION

National Society for Autistic Children
621 Central Avenue
Albany, New York 12206
   Approximately seventy local chapters.

HISTORY OF ASSOCIATION

The publication of "Infantile Autism" by Dr. Bernard Rimland, a psychologist and parent of an autistic child, and a television show called "Conall," a story of an autistic boy as told by his family, were two events which were historically important for autistic children. Hundreds of parents who saw the program or read the book wrote to Dr. Rimland.

In 1965, Dr. Rimland arranged meetings in Teaneck, New Jersey, and in Washington, D.C., inviting parents within a day's driving distance of each city. The overwhelming decision was that there should be a national organization which would work for the welfare of all children with severe behavioral disorders.

SERVICES OF NATIONAL HEADQUARTERS

The national headquarters makes referrals to local chapters and special institutions and programs. The Society works to bring into being programs of legislation, education and research for the benefit of all mentally ill children. Its newsletter serves as a vehicle for the exchange of the latest developments, legislation, schools, camps, and recreational services.

SERVICES OF AFFILIATES

Services vary from chapter to chapter. However, all make referrals to community resources. Parent and professional education are part of the program in most chapters. All chapters work to get special programs for autistic children in public schools.

PUBLICATIONS/FILMS

The publications of the Society include pamphlets such as "Children Apart" (50¢) and "The Lost Child" (20¢). A wide range of publications and bibliographies dealing with autism and related subjects are available.

RECREATION Affiliates organize recreation or encourage community groups, such as Girl and Boy Scouts, day camps, and residential camps to take a few autistic children.

STATE MENTAL HEALTH SERVICES

The National Institute of Mental Health estimates that approximately only five percent of the children in the United States who need psychiatric help are getting it; and of those who are treated, less than one-half receive help that is of the kind, quality, and duration needed.

Adequate facilities for children, facilities which provide a continuity and variety of services, are lacking in most areas of the country. However, through a national mental health program providing Federal support for the construction and staffing of community mental health centers, comprehensive mental health services are being made available throughout the country, in many areas for the first time.

DESCRIPTION OF SERVICES Facilities for services range from store-front neighborhood service centers in urban areas to regional or community treatment centers equipped with cottages for residential care. Centers reflect the special resources and needs of the community. Services are available to all regardless of ability to pay.

In order to qualify for federal funds, a center must provide at least five essential services:

1. Inpatient care—treatment to patients who need twenty-four-hour hospitalization.
2. Outpatient care—offers patients individual, group, or family therapy while permitting them to live at home.
3. Partial hospitalization—offers either day care for patients able to return home evenings, or night care for patients able to work but in need of further care and who

are usually without suitable home arrangements. It may include both day and night care and/or weekend care.

4. Emergency care—emergency psychiatric services at any hour around-the-clock, in one of the three units mentioned.

5. Consultation and education—made available by the center staff to community agencies and professional personnel.

A center may offer the following services in addition to the basic five, for a full, comprehensive program:

Diagnostic evaluation and recommendations for appropriate care.

Social and vocational counseling and rehabilitation.

Screening of patients prior to hospital admission, home visiting before and after hospitalization, and follow-up services for patients at outpatient clinics, in foster homes, or halfway houses.

Training programs for all types of mental health personnel.

Special services may be offered for children, alcoholics, or the retarded. Other special services may help to solve community problems such as drug abuse, suicide, or juvenile delinquency.

Some centers undertake research and evaluation to determine the effectiveness of their programs.

To learn about the mental health facilities in a community, write or call the state mental health authority or the state mental health association listed on pages 140–146.

STATE MENTAL HEALTH AUTHORITY AND STATE MENTAL HEALTH ASSOCIATIONS

All state associations of the organization are listed below the state mental authority, except where there is no affiliate.

ALABAMA   State Mental Health Authority, Department of Mental Health, 502 Washington Avenue, Montgomery, Alabama, 36104

The Alabama Association for Mental Health, Inc., 901 18th Street, South Birmingham, Alabama, 35205

ALASKA   Alaska Department of Health and Welfare, Division of Mental Health, Pouch "H," Juneau, Alaska, 99801

Alaska Mental Health Association, 1135 West 8th Avenue, Anchorage, Alaska, 99501

ARIZONA   State Mental Health Authority, State Department of Health, State Office Building, 1624 West Adams Street, Phoenix, Arizona, 85007

Arizona Association for Mental Health, Inc., 341 West McDowell Road, Phoenix, Arizona, 85003

ARKANSAS   State Mental Health Authority, 4313 West Markham Street, Little Rock, Arkansas

Arkansas Association for Mental Health, Inc., 424 West 6th Street, Little Rock, Arkansas, 72202

CALIFORNIA   State Mental Health Authority, State Department of Mental Hygiene, 744 "P" Street, Sacramento, California, 95814

California Association for Mental Health, 901 "H" Street, Suite 212, Sacramento, California, 95814

COLORADO   State Mental Health Authority, Department of Institutions, 328 State Services Building, Denver, Colorado, 80203

Colorado Association for Mental Health, Inc., 1375 Delaware Street, Denver, Colorado, 80204

CONNECTICUT   State Mental Health Authority, State Department of Mental Health, 90 Washington Street, Hartford, Connecticut, 06115

Connecticut Association for Mental Health, Inc., 123 Tremont Street, Hartford, Connecticut, 06105

DELAWARE   State Mental Health Authority, Department of Health and Social Services, Administration Building, Delaware State Hospital, New Castle, Delaware, 19720

Mental Health Association of Delaware, Inc., 701 Shipley Street, Wilmington, Delaware, 19801

DISTRICT OF COLUMBIA   State Mental Health Authority, 300 Indiana Avenue, N.W., Washington, D.C., 20001

District of Columbia Association for Mental

Health, Inc., 3000 Connecticut Avenue, N.W., Suite 100, Washington, D.C., 20008

FLORIDA State Mental Health Authority, Department of Health and Rehabilitative Services, Division of Mental Health, Larson Building, 200 East Gaines Street, Tallahassee, Florida, 32304

Florida Association of Mental Health, Suite 207, Myrick Building, 132 East Colonial Drive, Orlando, Florida, 32801

GEORGIA State Mental Health Authority, Georgia Department of Public Health, State Office Building, 47 Trinity Avenue, S.W., Atlanta, Georgia, 30334

Georgia Association for Mental Health, Inc., 230 Peachtree Street, N.W., Suite 214, Atlanta, Georgia, 30303

GUAM State Mental Health Authority, Department of Public Health and Welfare, Government of Guam, P.O. Box 2816, Agana, Guam, 96910

HAWAII State Mental Health Authority, State Department of Health, P.O. Box 3378, Honolulu, Hawaii, 96801

Mental Health Association of Hawaii, 200 North Vineyard, Honolulu, Hawaii, 96817

IDAHO State Mental Health Authority, Idaho Department of Health, Statehouse, Boise, Idaho, 83701

Idaho Mental Health Association, Inc., 311 North 10th Street, Boise, Idaho, 83702

ILLINOIS State Mental Health Authority, State Department of Mental Health, 1500 State of Illinois Building, 160 North LaSalle Street, Chicago, Illinois, 60601

Illinois Association for Mental Health, Inc., 710 Reisch Building, Lincoln Square, Springfield, Illinois, 62701

INDIANA State Mental Health Authority, State Department of Mental Health, 1315 West Tenth Street, Indianapolis, Indiana, 46207

The Mental Health Association of Indiana, 1433 Meridan Street, Indianapolis, Indiana, 46202

IOWA State Mental Health Authority, Community Health Services, Psychopathic Hospital, 500 Newton Road, Iowa City, Iowa, 52241

(No affiliated association.)

KANSAS State Mental Health Authority, Division of Institutional Management, State Department of Social Welfare, State Office Building, Topeka, Kansas, 66612

Kansas Association for Mental Health, Inc., 4015 West 21st Street, Topeka, Kansas, 66604

KENTUCKY State Mental Health Authority, State Department of Mental Health, Division of Children's Services, P.O. Box 678, Frankfort, Kentucky, 40601

The Kentucky Association for Mental Health, Inc., Suite 104, 310 West Liberty Street, Louisville, Kentucky, 40202

LOUISIANA State Mental Health Authority, Louisiana Department of Hospitals, 655 North Fifth Street, Baton Rouge, Louisiana, 70804

Louisiana Association for Mental Health, 1528 Jackson Avenue, New Orleans, Louisiana, 70130

MAINE State Mental Health Authority, State Department of Mental Health and Corrections, State Office Building, Augusta, Maine, 04330

(No affiliated association.)

MARYLAND State Mental Health Authority, State Department of Mental Hygiene, State Board of Health and Mental Hygiene, State Office Building, 301 West Preston Street, Baltimore, Maryland, 21201

Maryland Association for Mental Health, 325 East 25th Street, Baltimore, Maryland, 21218

MASSACHUSETTS State Mental Health Authority, State Department of Mental Health, Division of Children's Services, 190 Portland Street, Boston, Massachusetts, 02114

Massachusetts Association for Mental Health, Inc., 38 Chauncey Street, Room 801, Boston, Massachusetts

MICHIGAN State Mental Health Authority, State Department of Mental Health, Lewis Cass Building, Lansing, Michigan, 48913

Michigan Society for Mental Health, Inc., 27208 Southfield Road, Lathrup, Michigan, 48075

MINNESOTA State Mental Health Authority, State Department of Public Welfare, Centennial Building, St. Paul, Minnesota, 55101

Minnesota Association for Mental Health, Inc., 4510 West 77th Street, Room 100, Minneapolis, Minnesota, 55435

MISSISSIPPI	State Mental Health Authority, Felix Underwood Building, Jackson, Mississippi, 39201
	Mississippi Association for Mental Health, 902–904 Standard Life Building, Box 2081, Jackson, Mississippi, 39205
MISSOURI	State Mental Health Authority, State Department of Public Health and Welfare, Community Mental Health Services, 722 Jefferson Street, Jefferson City, Missouri, 65102
	Missouri Association for Mental Health, 411 Madison Avenue, Jefferson City, Missouri, 65101
MONTANA	State Mental Health Authority, State Division of Mental Hygiene, Montana State Hospital, Warm Springs, Montana, 59756
	Montana Association for Mental Health, Room 325, Wheat Building, Helena, Montana, 59601
NEBRASKA	State Mental Health Authority, State Department of Health, State Office Building, Lincoln, Nebraska, 68509
	(No affiliated association.)
NEVADA	State Mental Health Authority, State Department of Health and Welfare, 201 South Fall Street, Nye Building, Carson City, Nevada
	Nevada Association for Mental Health, Inc., 2018 East Charleston Boulevard, Las Vegas, Nevada, 89104
NEW HAMPSHIRE	Division of Mental Hygiene, Department of Health and Welfare, State House Annex, 105 Pleasant Street, Concord, New Hampshire, 03301
	(No affiliated association.)
NEW JERSEY	State Mental Health Authority, State Department of Institutions and Agencies, State Office Building, 135 West Hanover Street, Trenton, New Jersey, 08618
	The New Jersey Association for Mental Health, Inc., 60 South Fullerton Avenue, Montclair, New Jersey, 07042
NEW MEXICO	State Mental Health Authority, State Department of Public Health, 408 Galisteo Street, Santa Fe, New Mexico, 87501
	New Mexico Association for Mental Health, P.O. Drawer R, Santa Fe, New Mexico, 87501
NEW YORK	State Department of Mental Hygiene, 44 Holland Avenue, Albany, New York, 12208

The New York State Association for Mental Health, Inc., 90 State Street, Albany, New York, 12207

NORTH CAROLINA State Department of Mental Health, 441 North Harrington Street, P.O. Box 9494, Raleigh, North Carolina, 27603

North Carolina Mental Health Association, 425 North Boylan Avenue, Raleigh, North Carolina, 27603

NORTH DAKOTA State Mental Health Authority, State Department of Health, State Capitol, Bismarck, North Dakota, 58501

North Dakota Mental Health Association, P.O. Box 160, 202½ North Third Street, Bismarck, North Dakota, 58501

OHIO State Mental Health Authority, State Department of Mental Hygiene and Correction, State Office Building, Columbus, Ohio, 43215

Mental Health Federation, Inc., Ohio Division, M-59 The Neil House Hotel, Columbus, Ohio, 43215

OKLAHOMA State Department of Mental Health, State Capitol Building, Oklahoma City, Oklahoma, 73105

The Oklahoma Association for Mental Health, Inc., 3113 Classen Boulevard, Oklahoma City, Oklahoma, 73118

OREGON State Mental Health Division, 2570 Center Street N.E., Salem, Oregon, 97310

Mental Health Association of Oregon, 718 West Burnside Street, Room 504, Portland, Oregon, 97209

PENNSYLVANIA State Mental Health Authority, State Department of Public Welfare, Health and Welfare Building, Harrisburg, Pennsylvania, 17120

Pennsylvania Mental Health, Inc., 1207 Chestnut Street, Philadelphia, Pennsylvania, 19103

PUERTO RICO State Mental Health Authority, Puerto Rico Department of Health, Ponce de Leon Avenue, San Juan, Puerto Rico, 00918

(No affiliated association.)

RHODE ISLAND State Mental Health Authority, Department of Mental Health, Retardation and Hospitals, 1 Washington Avenue, Providence, Rhode Island, 02905

Rhode Island Association for Mental Health, Inc., 333 Grotto Avenue, Providence, Rhode Island, 02906

SOUTH CAROLINA State Mental Health Authority, State Department of Mental Health, 2214 Bull Street, Columbia, South Carolina, 29201

South Carolina Mental Health Association, 1823 Gadsen Street, Columbia, South Carolina, 29201

SOUTH DAKOTA State Mental Health Authority, State Commission of Mental Health and Mental Retardation, Yankton State Hospital, Yankton, South Dakota, 57078

South Dakota Mental Health Association, 101½ South Pierre Street, Box 355, Pierre, South Dakota, 57501

TENNESSEE State Mental Health Authority, State Department of Mental Health, 300 Cordell Hull Building, Nashville, Tennessee, 37219

Tennessee Mental Health Association, 1717 West End Building, Suite 421, Nashville, Tennessee, 37203

TEXAS State Mental Health Authority, State Department of Mental Health and Mental Retardation, Box S, Capitol Station, Austin, Texas, 78711

The Texas Association for Mental Health, 107 Lantern Lane, Austin, Texas, 78731

UTAH State Mental Health Authority, Division of Mental Health, Utah Department of Social Services, 520 East Fourth South, Salt Lake City, Utah, 84102

Utah Association for Mental Health, 211 East Third South, Suite 212, Salt Lake City, Utah, 84111

VERMONT State Mental Health Authority, State Department of Mental Health, State Office Building, Montpelier, Vermont, 05602

(No affiliated association.)

VIRGIN ISLANDS State Mental Health Authority, Department of Health, Charlotte Amalie, St. Thomas, Virgin Island, 00801

(No affiliated association.)

VIRGINIA State Mental Health Authority, State Department of Mental Hygiene and Hospitals, P.O. Box 1797, Richmond, Virginia, 23214

	Virginia Association for Mental Health, Inc., 2 North First Street, Richmond, Virginia, 23219
WASHINGTON	State Mental Health Authority, State Department of Health, Public Health Building, Olympia, Washington, 98501
	Washington Association for Mental Health, c/o Mrs. Ruth Coffin, 1308 72nd Avenue, Yakima, Washington, 98902
WEST VIRGINIA	State Mental Health Authority, State Department of Mental Health, 922 Quarrier Street, Charleston, West Virginia, 25305
	West Virginia Association for Mental Health, Inc., 815 Quarrier Street, 318 Morrison Building, Charleston, West Virginia, 25301
WISCONSIN	State Mental Health Authority, State Department of Public Welfare, 1 West Wilson Street, Madison, Wisconsin, 53702
	Wisconsin Association for Mental Health, 119 East Mifflin, P.O. Box 1486, Madison, Wisconsin, 53701
WYOMING	State Mental Health Authority, State Department of Public Health, State Office Building, Cheyenne, Wyoming, 82001
	Wyoming Association for Mental Health, c/o Mrs. Norman Stark, 1417 West 6th Avenue, Cheyenne, Wyoming, 82001

NATIONAL ASSOCIATION FOR MENTAL HEALTH

The National Association for Mental Health (NAMH), 1800 North Kent Street, Rosslyn Station, Arlington, Virginia, 22209, is a national citizens' voluntary organization with divisions and chapters throughout the country. The association is not connected with any government agency, but is a source of information on both private and public mental health facilities.

Muscular Dystrophy

DESCRIPTION OF CONDITION

Muscular dystrophy is the name given a group of chronic, noncontagious progressive diseases having certain important features in common and others that distinguish the different types from one another. The prominent characteristic shared by all of them is the progressive wasting —slow in some types and relatively fast in others —of the voluntary muscles, a process which leads to increasing infirmity and, ultimately, to death. Nearly two-thirds of the known muscular dystrophy victims in the United States are children between the ages of three and fifteen.

Although the precise cause of muscular dystrophy has not yet been determined, it appears to be the result of an inborn error of metabolism, the lack of some specific enzyme system essential for the conversion of foods into tissues and energy. For the most part, patients come from families with a history of muscular dystrophy, although spontaneous occurrence as the result of genetic mutation is not uncommon. The hereditary defect may be transmitted by either parent.

The primary pathology, in all types of dystrophy, appears to lie in the muscle cell itself, with the nervous system involved only indirectly, if at all. There are variations in the age of onset, in the muscle groups first affected, and in the rate of progression.

There are four main types of muscular dystrophy: *the pseudohypertrophic (Duchenne) type*, which is the most prevalent form; *the juvenile form*, which has its onset in childhood; *the facioscapulo humeral form*, which affects the facial muscles, shoulders, and upper arms; and *limb girdle*, a condition which has its onset between the ages of thirty and fifty.

TREATMENT

No treatment has yet been found to correct the underlying pathology nor to arrest the relentless progression of the disease. As the muscles deteriorate, the patient becomes weak and helpless.

Isolated claims of temporary beneficial effects have been reported with a wide variety of diets and substances. None has been shown to have any significant lasting effect on the course of the disease.

Physical therapy has proven of limited value in delaying the onset of contractures but does not otherwise affect the course of the dystrophic process.

Antibiotics prolong the lives of many children who would otherwise succumb to respiratory infections, but have no curative effect on muscular dystrophy.

PROGNOSIS The rate of progression varies in the different types of dystrophy. Generally, the earlier clinical symptoms appear, the more rapid is the progression. As the muscles deteriorate, the patient becomes weaker and more helpless, and is unable to carry out the simplest activities of everyday life. Death usually results from respiratory failure; however, it may be precipitated by involvement of the heart muscles.

MEDICAL PROGRESS For the first time, hereditary muscular dystrophy has been reversed in an animal species. This development, involving a strain of chicken with a genetic defect, was achieved by scientists at the Institute for Muscle Disease, a research center sponsored by Muscular Dystrophy Associations of America. Although the various types of muscular dystrophy in humans are similarly caused by a genetic defect, scientists do not know how closely the causative mechanisms in the chickens are related with those in human beings —or if the syndromes are identical. They both share the prominent features of muscular dystrophy inheritance; muscle wasting that is progressive and without spontaneous reversal; deposition of large amounts of fat replacing the wasted muscle; and characteristic changes in biochemistry. By understanding the disease in other species, it is hoped the findings may some day provide a basis for an approach to the management of the disorder in human beings.

FUTURE MEDICAL GOALS Many scientists believe that in the future the idea of replacing or regulating defective genes may be realized. The foundation has been laid for the deciphering of the genetic code. The primary bearer of the code which dictates hereditary characteristics is DNA (deoxyribonucleic acid), the chemical material found in the nucleus of every living cell; it is believed that a gene is a segment of one of the molecules of DNA. RNA (ribonucleic acid), which is found both in and out of the cell nucleus, transmits and helps to carry out the DNA's instructions for manufacturing proteins, including enzymes, in the cell. Many studies are pointing toward eventual control of these all-important nucleic acids. Differences between the RNAs of normal and dystrophic muscles have been identified in studies of mice. Before any attempt can be made to alter abnormal human RNA to enable it to produce its regular complement of enzymes, however, similar studies of normal and dystrophic human muscle must be carried out.

DRUG THERAPY There are no drugs currently known which have any effect upon the underlying pathology of muscular dystrophy—or which can stop the progression of the disease.

TESTS Since the dystrophies and most related diseases are genetically determined, knowledge of other cases in different generations of the same family helps to confirm a diagnosis. A family history is taken, in addition to the routine physical examination. A *biopsy*, a small thin slice of tissue from a weakened muscle is chemically stained with special dyes and then studied under the microscope. Dystrophic muscle, as seen microscopically, has a characteristically abnormal appearance.

One widely used test is an *electromyogram*, similar to an electrocardiogram, except that electrodes are placed in suspected dystrophic muscle groups. Characteristic readings of dystrophic muscles register somewhat reduced voltage on the electromyogram.

Another test frequently given is called the *creatine test*. When muscles waste, the substances they are unable to metabolize accumulate in the blood and urine. A high urinary output of unused *creatine* (an amino acid derivative normally deposited in voluntary muscles) and a low urinary output of *creatinine* (the waste product which normally results from the metabolism of creatine) are good indications of disturbed muscle metabolism.

The serum enzyme test is helpful for early diagnosis, since the serum content of enzymes is abnormally increased very early in the course of dystrophy, long before any clinical symptoms appear. When a muscle is normal, all constituents of the cell are retained within its membrane. In dystrophy, where muscle tissue breaks down, the membrane becomes unusually permeable and substances originally contained within the cell escape into the blood serum, and can be found there at levels higher than normal.

Various tests have been developed for identifying carriers of the most common and severe type of dystrophy, the Duchenne or pseudohypertrophic, which is transmitted on a sex-linked recessive gene. These tests are based on the fact that the pathological process is present to some degree in the majority of carriers even though they may be totally lacking in clinical symptoms. (As much as fifty percent of muscle mass may be lost before such symptoms become apparent.)

The most reliable of these tests—with an effectiveness of approximately seventy to eighty percent—is the CPK serum enzyme determination used in pre-clinical diagnosis. Since CPK levels decrease with age, its accuracy is greater in young girls than in older women. In borderline cases, electromyography and/or biopsy may be used to confirm tentative findings.

NOTE: Facilities for female carrier testing are available at most Muscular Dystrophy Associations of America clinics. They also offer, when it is requested, expert counsel on family planning.

SERVICES

SPECIALISTS The Muscular Dystrophy Associations' eighty-five out-patient clinics provide comprehensive diagnostic and follow-up services. The team of medical specialists includes neurologists, orthopedists, pediatric neurologists, and *physiatrists* (physicians who direct physical therapy). Specialists in many other disciplines are involved in the basic research aspects of the disease. They include geneticists, biologists, and biochemists.

COMMUNITY HEALTH INFORMATION The 325 chapters of Muscular Dystrophy Associations in fifty states, the District of Columbia, Puerto Rico, and Guam are the best sources of information on community resources and facilities for muscular dystrophy and related neuromuscular diseases.

STATE HEALTH SERVICES Every crippled children's agency has its own range of services. All states include diagnostic services and treatment for children with muscular dystrophy and related neuromuscular diseases or make arrangements for youngsters nearby.

FEDERAL RESEARCH PROGRAM The National Institute of Neurological Diseases and Stroke coordinates the research on the causes, prevention, diagnosis, and treatment of the neurological, sensory, and communicative disorders. More than 200 clinical disabilities associated with dysfunction, disease, or injury of the nervous system are the concern of the Institute. See page 203 for a description of the scope of research.

VOLUNTARY HEALTH ASSOCIATION Muscular Dystrophy Associations of America, Inc.
1790 Broadway
New York, N.Y. 10019
There are 325 chapters throughout all the fifty states, the District of Columbia, Puerto Rico, and Guam.

HISTORY OF ASSOCIATION

As late as 1950, very little was being done about dystrophy. In that year Muscular Dystrophy Associations of America, Inc., was formed by a small group of parents in New York whose children had been stricken by the disease. One of the few scientists concerned with the problem at that time was Dr. Ade T. Milhorat, Professor of Clinical Medicine at Cornell University Medical College. The group of parents sought him out for advice before organizing the Association and later appointed him as chairman of its Medical Advisory Board. Almost immediately after the Association was founded, chapter affiliates were created in all parts of the country.

In the summer of 1959, a major new research center, the Institute for Muscle Disease, opened in New York. Built and supported by the Association, the Institute serves as headquarters for a concentrated scientific attack on muscular dystrophy, as well as related neuromuscular disorders.

SERVICES OF NATIONAL HEADQUARTERS

Services include: direct payment for all authorized services for patients who live in areas where there are no chapters; referral of patients who do live in chapter areas to the appropriate affiliate for services; mass media promotion to educate the public about muscular dystrophy and related conditions; the creation and distribution of lay and professional literature and films; the sponsoring of national and international research conferences.

SERVICES OF LOCAL AFFILIATES

All chapters provide payment in full for certain authorized direct services, which include: purchase and repair of orthopedic appliances prescribed by a physician; physical therapy; transportation, if possible, to and from clinics, recreational events; influenza shots when recommended by local physicians; summer camp referral.

In urban centers throughout the nation, and

in a number of smaller cities as well, out-patient clinics offer diagnostic services and follow-up visits. (Costs of all the medical services and laboratory tests required for diagnosis are paid for either by a chapter or by the Association in areas where there are no chapters.)

In areas where there are no Muscular Dystrophy Associations clinics, chapters pay for treatment by local physicians of patients suffering from the disease entities covered by the program. These include, in addition to the muscular dystrophies, certain other noninfectious neuromuscular disorders.

PUBLICATIONS

Individual fact sheets are available on each disease treated in the clinics. They include:

1) Muscular Dystrophy (various forms)

2) Infantile Spinal Muscular Atrophy (Werdnig-Hoffman Disease)

3) Benign Congenital Hypotonia (Oppenheim's Disease)

4) Juvenile Spinal Muscular Atrophy (Kugelberg-Welander Disease)

5) Spinal Muscular Atrophy of Adults (Aran-Duchenne Type)

6) Amyotrophic Lateral Sclerosis

7) Peroneal Muscular Atrophy (Charcot-Marie-Tooth Disease)

FILMS

"The Sun Never Sets," awarded honors at the American Film Festival as top film in its class, depicts the worldwide scientific battle against muscular dystrophy by showing one day in the life of a young patient. Other films are available on a loan basis, although quantities are extremely limited. Write National Headquarters for a list of films.

A medical teaching film, "Muscular Dystrophy

and Related Conditions: Differential Diagnosis," is available on loan at no charge to medical schools and professional groups.

EDUCATION

Chapters work with local elementary and secondary school authorities for the inclusion of children with dystrophy and related disease in existing educational programs. Wherever possible, transportation is provided.

RECREATION

Some chapters provide recreational programs, ranging from supervised excursions to organized group activities such as summer camps.

VOCABULARY

Collagen —Connective tissue which together with fat replaces protein in the various forms of muscular dystrophy.

Creatine —An amino acid derivative normally deposited in voluntary muscle. When creatine is metabolized the waste product creatinine is found in the urine. In disease of muscle wasting such as dystrophy, muscle does not accept or retain creatine and there is an elevated level of creatine in the urine.

Dystrophy —Weakness and degeneration of muscle which is primary and not resulting from nerve damage.

Voluntary muscles —All the muscles in the body in which there is conscious control over contraction.

Orthopedic and Physically Handicapping Conditions

SEE THE FOLLOWING CATEGORIES: Arthritis
Birth Defects
Cerebral Palsy
Hemophilia
Muscular Dystrophy

State Crippled Children's Program (page 189); The National Foundation (page 25); and the National Society for Crippled Children and Adults (page 27) are sources of information, provide diagnosis, and treat a wide variety of congenital and acquired conditions. Dislocated hips, complicated fractures, diseases of the bone, bow legs, foot deformities, and scoliosis are among the conditions treated.

Birthmarks, webbed fingers or toes, as well as certain other skin malformations of face and body and acute burns or complications from old burns are treated as well.

Some states, as part of their physical restoration programs, provide hospitalization, surgery, braces, and other orthopedic appliances and transportation to clinics to those who are eligible.

Retardation

The American Association on Mental Deficiency describes mental retardation as significant "subaverage general intellectual functioning which originates during the developmental period and is associated with impairment in adaptive behavior."

There are between 100,000 and 200,000 babies born each year who are to some extent retarded or become retarded. The degree of retardation ranges from the mildly affected who, with special training and guidance, can achieve a state of self-sufficiency as adults, to those profoundly retarded who can learn basic self-care and profit significantly from training in behavioral control, self-protection, language development and physical mobility.

Mildly Retarded: Approximately eighty-nine percent of this country's mentally retarded citizens are mildly retarded, having Stanford-Binet IQs of 52 to 67. Mildly retarded persons are highly similar to their nonretarded peers, differing primarily only in rate and degree of intellectual development. On this level, retardation is not readily apparent, and children are not usually identified as retarded until they enter school. During adulthood, they again tend to lose their identity as mentally retarded when they are absorbed into the competitive labor market and daily community life. Educational programs for the mildly retarded of all ages—up to and including adulthood—should be designed to maximize social, educational, and vocational skills relevant to independent community living and gainful employment.

Neglect of handicapping conditions in a child's environment during the preschool period is particularly critical for later development. Preschool programs should emphasize a variety of perceptual, cognitive, and social learning experiences combined with self-care, language, and physical development. If possible, mildly retarded school-aged residents of institutions should be enrolled in appropriate school classes, preferably in the community public school system. In special schools and classes the educational curriculum is directly related to the problems the individual will be likely to encounter in independent living situations.

Moderately Retarded: Moderately retarded persons account for approximately six percent of the retarded population, having Stanford-Binet IQs from 31 to 51. In the last decade, increasing emphasis has been placed upon the role of families, public schools, and community agencies in the training and habilitation of moderately retarded persons. Community-based training programs have shown that moderately retarded citizens can live acceptably in group homes and make valuable social and occupational contributions through employment in sheltered workshops or other supervised work settings.

The developmental delay exhibited by moderately retarded children is not as pronounced as with profoundly and severely retarded persons, but their unusual slowness in sitting alone, standing, walking, and learning to talk is obvious to most parents. Preschool training includes toilet training, simple dressing, self-feeding, and social adjustments. School programs include self-direction, practical reading and writing, social adjustment, communication, and pre-work training, and they are made to be highly relevant to daily life.

Severely Retarded: Approximately three-and-one-half percent of the estimated 6.1 million mentally retarded persons in the United States are severely retarded. Their pronounced developmental delay is highly similar during early life to profoundly retarded children, although their rate of progress and development potential are significantly greater.

Because severely retarded infants may experience several years of marked physical immobility and minimal responsiveness to their surroundings, the environment in which they live must include a planned variety of visual experiences, sounds, gentle handling, and other opportunities to use all senses. It is important as well to provide a variety of out-of-bed areas for mat or water play, eating, and other daily activities; the child's surroundings should be furnished with toys, wall decorations, mobiles, and other stimuli to attract interest and attention. Educational programs must insure optimal physical development and provide an environment conducive to learning skills, including self-feeding, dressing, bathing, toilet use, language development, and social responsiveness. Training begun in the preschool period must be continued on an intensive basis during early school-age years in order to help severely retarded youngsters to require less care and supervision.

Profoundly Retarded: The profoundly retarded represent the most extreme degree of mental retardation (IQs below 20), accounting for one-and-one-half percent of all mentally retarded persons. Systematic training efforts have clearly demonstrated that, with exceedingly few exceptions, profoundly retarded persons can profit considerably from training in such areas as self-care, language development, self-protection, impulse control, and physical mobility.

It is imperative that profoundly retarded infants be allowed a variety of body positions, receive passive exercise, and move about whenever possible. Their living environment should include a planned variety of stimuli to afford them frequent opportunities for using all senses.

If opportunity and encouragement to develop optimally are provided during the first years of life, young school-age profoundly retarded residents will be prepared for active training in self-care including self-feeding, dressing, bathing, and toilet use. Training programs may also incorporate language development activities, physical fitness, personal control, and self-direction.

Although over 200 specific conditions have been discovered, no clear determination of cause can be made in seventy-five to eighty-five percent of the identified cases of mental retardation.

Among specific causes are German measles (rubella) in the mother during the first three months of pregnancy; meningitis, toxoplasmosis; Rh-factor incompatability between mother and infant; lead poisoning in young children; chromosomal abnormalities. Also, untreated inborn errors of metabolism can cause damage to the central nervous system, and physical malformations of the brain or other organs can result in mental retardation.

Prenatal care can be a crucial factor in preventing retardation. However, even today, approximately thirty percent of the expectant mothers in the United States receive no prenatal care at all—and many who do see a physician are not fully aware of the importance of his instructions.

The disproportionately high incidence of mental retardation in poverty areas in conjunction with research on the effects of cultural deprivation suggests that contributing factors to mental retardation may be mother and child malnutrition, chronic disease-producing surroundings, restricted opportunities for learning, and the generally harsh living conditions associated with life in disadvantaged environments. Children in these areas are also often deprived of the stimuli of touch, talk, shared activity, and encouragement that are essential to growth and learning.

EDUCATION AND TRAINING

Mental retardation is not a specific disease or disorder but a complex of mental and social limitations. Consequently, the services of a variety of specialists, particularly educators, psychologists, social workers, physicians, nurses, counselors and therapists are necessary for evaluation and training program design.

The physician treating a mentally retarded child, the local chapter of the Association for Retarded Children, or the State Health Department, can make referral to available facilities in the public school system, vocational rehabilitation, speech and hearing training—all important in the treatment of the retarded. Mental health clinics, family counseling agencies, or out-patient clinics for the retarded are available in some communities and are helpful to both child and parent.

Of prime importance in the prevention of mental retardation is the health of the mother before and during pregnancy; constant attention to the development of the child from the embryonic stage through delivery; and the assurance that once born, the child is given the chance to become physically strong and the opportunity to learn and to experience sensory and cultural stimulation.

Special education is necessary for the retarded child. The President's Committee on Mental Retardation has concluded that less than half of the 1,200,000 mentally retarded youngsters in the United States are receiving educational services. Services are available predominantly in New England, the East, and Far West and are least likely to be available in the Southwest, Southeast, and the Plains States.

PROGNOSIS At the present time approximately three percent of the population is mentally retarded. The majority are classified as mildly retarded and are capable, with special schooling and training, of being self-supporting through productive employment by the time chronological adulthood is reached. The next two groups, the moderately and severely retarded, can function well as adults in sheltered living environments and workshop settings offering specialized training and supervision to develop their limited skills. The profoundly retarded, who at one time were thought not to be capable of any achievement, can be taught to manage basic self-help skills, such as feeding or dressing. Increased attention to the retarded has made the prognosis hopeful.

DRUG THERAPY There are no specific drugs to ameliorate this condition. Drugs do have a place in the management of many retarded persons. Anticonvulsants are used for seizures; tranquilizers or amphetamines, to reduce hyperactivity and increase attention spans. Drug therapy must be determined on an individual basis by the treating physician.

TESTS   Adequate training and care are dependent on early detection and evaluation. Severe mental retardation is usually detected at birth or during infancy. But during infancy the majority of more mildly affected children at first seem quite normal and are not readily identifiable. A doctor observing a child over a period of time may note a lag in growth and development, but the majority of the retarded are not identified until they begin school. A variety of diagnostic tests are used to evaluate intelligence and social adaptation and to arrive at an effective training program for the individual child.

SERVICES

SPECIALISTS   Pediatricians, neurologists, social workers, psychologists, special educational, and vocational counselors in addition to paramedical personnel such as physical and occupational therapists, audiologists, and public health nurses are all concerned with this problem.

COMMUNITY HEALTH INFORMATION   State and local associations for the retarded are generally member units of the National Association for Retarded Children. They are listed in the telephone directory by county, city (e.g., Dallas Association for Retarded Children), or state name. Some may be listed as "Association for Help of the Retarded."

STATE HEALTH SERVICES   In the past, crippled children's agencies provided care for more children with handicaps needing orthopedic or plastic treatment than children with other kinds of crippling conditions. States have increasingly broadened their programs to include children with any kind of handicapping conditions, including physically handicapped children who are also mentally retarded. See pages 189–196 for a list of state agencies which provide these services.

FEDERAL RESEARCH PROGRAM

Several Institutes of Health have conducted research related to mental retardation. The National Institute of Neurological Diseases and Stroke conducts studies related to mental retardation and supports studies at other institutions. A large source of federal support to retardation has come from the Social Rehabilitation Services Administration of the Department of Health, Education, and Welfare.

VOLUNTARY HEALTH ASSOCIATION

National Association for Retarded Children
2709 Avenue "E"
East Arlington, Texas 76011
    There are 1,500 local units in fifty states, the District of Columbia and Puerto Rico.

HISTORY OF ASSOCIATION
The National Association for Retarded Children was organized in 1950 as the National Association of Parents and Friends of Mentally Retarded Children and incorporated under its current name in 1953. This organization devotes itself to the problem of retardation through the advancement of research, community services, improved facilities, and educational programs, as well as broader public understanding of the problem of mental retardation.

SERVICES OF NATIONAL HEADQUARTERS
Does not make referrals, but supplies general information with respect to programs, facilities, institutions, and careers for the retarded. Requests for referral are generally directed to the local chapters and their diagnostic centers, or to other agencies specializing in this field.

SERVICES OF LOCAL AFFILIATES
Local chapters are encouraged to promote, but not to provide direct services to the retarded.

Many of the older chapters have large-scale programs in terms of educational facilities, sheltered workshops, camps, and recreational programs. The majority have referral services and information for parents or public educational services.

PUBLICATIONS/FILMS
Publications include a wide range of literature for parents and professionals. There are such pamphlets as:
"Into the Light of Learning"
"Primer for Parents of a Mentally Retarded Child"
"Facts on Mental Retardation"
"A Fresh Look at Retarded Children"
"How Children Develop Intellectually"
Other pamphlets are available on such topics as education, recreation, vocational rehabilitation and residential care for the mentally retarded. A complete list is available without charge.

RELIGIOUS AFFILIATES Referrals are made by local chapters and some religious organizations have residential facilities for the retarded. See page 184 for information on religious affiliated organizations.

Various religious agencies have in- and outpatient facilities. Contact your local chapter or the social service department of the various religious agencies.

VOCABULARY

Anoxia —Insufficient oxygen supply to tissues of the body.

Hydrocephalus —A condition which results from an abnormal collection of fluid within the cavities of the brain.

Kernicterus —A condition resulting from blood incompatability involving the Rh blood factor which may result in mental retardation; jaundice occurs in the medulla oblongata.

Microcephalus —A condition in which the skull and brain are abnormally small.

Rubella (German measles) —May cause birth defects including retardation, cataracts, heart defects, and deafness if mother contracts disease during first three months of pregnancy.

Sickle-Cell Anemia

DESCRIPTION OF CONDITION An editorial in a recent issue of *The New England Journal of Medicine* called sickle-cell anemia "possibly the most neglected major health problem in the nation today." There are over two million Black Americans in this country with sickle-cell disease.

Sickle-cell anemia is an incurable inherited disorder which occurs in the severe form in one out of every 400 Black Americans, and in the mild form, or trait, in one out of every ten Black Americans.

Sickle-cell anemia results when a child inherits two sickle-cell genes—one from each parent—that cause the production of an abnormal form of the blood protein hemoglobin. Hemoglobin, contained in the red blood cells, serves as a carrier of oxygen to body tissues.

Normally, red blood cells are shaped like a doughnut with a hole that does not go through completely. In the sickle-cell disease process, the red blood cells take on an abnormal sickle, or crescent, shape.

In a child with sickle-cell anemia, the oxygen-carrying capacity of the blood is impaired and the sickle-shaped red blood cells tend to clog small capillaries, causing blood occlusion and depriving tissues of oxygen. The patient suffers frequent bouts of pain and chronic fatigue. Ordinary physical activity is limited, and the entire educational program must be geared to the individual's physical capabilities.

TREATMENT There is no known medical cure for sickle-cell anemia. A physician can only prescribe to relieve the symptoms or to prevent complications. Frequent blood transfusions are necessary to counteract and replace destroyed red blood cells.

The body processes which would destroy a normal red blood cell in about 120 days often destroy a sickle cell in a fraction of that time. Although new red blood cells are produced the body cannot match the destruction of old cells with new ones.

Generally, when a sickle-cell patient has a *thrombotic crisis* (i.e., pains in extremities, abdomen), the methods used are supportive. They include bed rest, analgesics, sedation, and hydration. When infection accompanies such a crisis, appropriate antibiotics are prescribed. Folic acid and multivitamins are given by some clinics to some patients as a kind of prophylaxis. Folic acid is known to provide some small stimulation to the bone marrow.

PROGNOSIS

The prognosis is not good. Patients afflicted with severe forms of the disease usually die in childhood or early adult life. However, various clinics across the country have reported extended lifespans with a few patients.

Regular clinic care can help patients live longer because infections may be treated at the onset; sometimes prophylactic transfusions and other types of supportive care are given.

MEDICAL PROGRESS

Many drugs have been tried in various clinics with different degrees of success. It is important to note, however, that there has not been a real breakthrough. At the present time research has been conducted to determine the effect of a drug known as urea that may be useful in the unsickling of the red blood cells and the alleviation of pain.

For the most part the methods are essentially all aimed at relieving symptoms and treating complications, but not treating the basic defect of the disease, which is a genetic one.

FUTURE GOALS

Research is being conducted into treatment methods which may reduce or do away with the sickling phenomenon.

TESTS

When screening patients, the same basic diagnostic test is given to all. The sickling phenomenon is detected by exposing the patient's blood to a low oxygen tension. If the blood cells assume a "sickle" shape, it is due to the presence of an abnormal hemoglobin.

A further test is made to determine whether the person has the severe form of the disease or has a sickle-cell trait, or whether the person is a carrier of the disease.

SERVICES

SPECIALISTS   Pediatricians, hemotologists, and general practitioners provide the first line of defense in the clinical care of the sickle-cell patient. Specialists of many other disciplines are involved in the basic research aspects of the disease, and specialized clinical management of the sickle-cell patient. They include geneticists; biologists, particularly molecular biologists; and biochemists. Specialized medical areas that may be involved in the care of the patient include neurology, urology, and ophthalmology.

COMMUNITY HEALTH INFORMATION   Community health resources vary from community to community. Screening for the sickling phenomenon is basic to any community health project involved with the disease. It is sometimes done in schools. Screening is also conducted by the Department of Health, Special Sickle Cell Foundation, in-patient hospital service, out-patient hospital service, and genetic counseling groups (particularly in urban areas).

RESEARCH FOUNDATION   The Foundation for Research and Education in Sickle Cell Disease, 421–431 West 120th Street, New York, N.Y., 10027, is a professional group concerned with the problems of the disease and with making the public aware of sickle-cell disease. A private organization, not funded by federal, state, or city funds, the Foundation depends on private contributions.

The Foundation has assisted in establishing special treatment clinics for treatment of sickle-cell anemia in the New York metropolitan area, but accepts requests for referrals throughout the United States.

VOCABULARY

Aplastic crisis —In which the bone marrow inadequately produces red blood cells. This type requires transfusion.

Crisis —A sudden intensification of symptoms in the course of sickle-cell anemia. The most frequent type of crisis is the "thrombotic" or "painful" crisis.

Hand-foot syndrome —Painful swelling of the hands and feet seen in young sufferers of sickle-cell anemia.

Hemoglobin electrophoresis —The specific test used to determine the kind of sickle-cell disease present in an individual.

Tay-Sachs Disease

DESCRIPTION OF CONDITION
Tay-Sachs disease is a hereditary metabolic disorder in which faulty enzymatic mechanisms doom infants to an early death. The disease was first described in 1881 by British ophthalmologist Warren Tay and then in 1887 by Dr. Bernard Sachs of Mount Sinai Hospital, New York.

The disease particularly strikes children of Jewish couples, with the highest frequency among descendants of Jews from the region of the pre–World War I Polish-Russian border.

In this country there are about 250 cases a year of Tay-Sachs disease and about 2,000 cases of the half-dozen related diseases in this group.

In a Tay-Sachs victim, there is a failure of the system to produce an enzyme essential to the chemical process within cells that metabolizes fats. As a result, excessive fats accumulate in the brain cells and block normal activity.

The cause of Tay-Sachs disease is now known. Recently research centers have identified the enzymatic defect associated with the disease. All implicate the same enzyme: hexosaminidase component A (hex-A). Continued research has now answered the question of whether it is this defective enzyme that causes the excessive accumulation of fats in Tay-Sachs disease: it does.

A parent who carries a single defective Tay-Sachs gene will not be afflicted with the disease himself. But if both parents carry a Tay-Sachs gene, there is a one-in-four risk that their baby will receive two abnormal genes—one from each parent—and be afflicted. If the child receives only one, his body will produce less hexosaminidase component A than it should, but he will be able to lead a normal life. Like his parents, he will be a healthy carrier.

TREATMENT
There is no effective therapy for Tay-Sachs Disease. The clinical symptoms of the disease usually begin to appear at six months. One of the earliest is an exaggeratedly startled reaction to

sound. Blindness, psychomotor deterioration, and progressive mental retardation follow invariably. The disease is always fatal; hospitalized patients average forty months of age at death.

TESTS The identification of hexosaminidase component A has enabled doctors to detect both the carriers and victims of Tay-Sachs Disease. If blood tests reveal that both a man and his wife have less than normal amounts of Hex-A and are, therefore, carriers of Tay-Sachs genes, they can be warned of their 25 percent risk of producing a Tay-Sachs child. They may, then, wish to have no children of their own; or they may elect pregnancy and submit to amniocentesis for prenatal diagnosis; or they may adopt a child.

Amniocentesis is used in prenatal diagnosis in several genetic diseases. Recently, because of the new research in identifying the enzymatic defect, amniocentesis has been applied to Tay-Sachs disease. By inserting a needle through a woman's abdomen when she is sixteen weeks pregnant and extracting a small amount of fluid for analysis from the amniotic sac, doctors can determine if the unborn child will have Tay-Sachs disease. Cells shed by the developing fetus into the fluid will be analyzed for traces of Hex-A.

SERVICES

SPECIALISTS Pediatricians and pediatric neurologists provide the clinical care for the Tay-Sachs child. Other specialists are involved in the basic research aspects of the disease, particularly biochemists, geneticists, and molecular biologists.

COMMUNITY HEALTH INFORMATION Community health resources are exceedingly limited throughout the United States. National Tay-Sachs and Allied Diseases Association and their affiliates make referrals.

VOLUNTARY HEALTH ASSOCIATION National Tay-Sachs and Allied Diseases Association, Inc.

200 Park Avenue South
New York, N.Y. 10003

There are seven affiliates in Metropolitan New York, New Jersey, Philadelphia, and Washington, D.C. New chapters are forming.

HISTORY OF ASSOCIATION

Five parents who had lost children with Tay-Sachs founded the Association in 1957. The Association has grown to seven affiliates concentrated in the East, who support research, programs of education, prevention and control and make referrals to services in all parts of the United States.

SERVICES OF ASSOCIATION

Both national headquarters and affiliates make referrals to clinics for diagnosis and carrier and prenatal detection throughout the United States. Information about social services and nursing care is also available.

VOCABULARY

Hyperacusia —Abnormal sensitivity to sound.

Muscular hypotonia —Limp quality of muscle.

Myoclonic seizures —Sometimes called lightning seizures; should be suspected in infants showing sudden jerks of the eyes and forearms or sudden transient loss of muscle tone with falling to the ground.

Tuberculosis

Before antituberculosis drugs were discovered in the 1940s, the only treatment of tuberculosis was usually a combination of rest, good food, fresh air and sometimes surgery.

The new medicines now reduce the spread of the disease. However, about 37,000 people a year still contract tuberculosis each year in the United States.

Some patients with tuberculosis live in rural areas, but the majority live in large cities, particularly in inner-city ghettos where health and hygienic standards are low.

Tuberculosis is a communicable disease caused by a germ, the tubercle bacillus (TB), first described by bacteriologist Robert Koch in 1882. TB is not hereditary. The TB germs are breathed in with air and so go first to the lungs, which are most commonly attacked by the disease. The disease may also be found in other parts of the body.

With early detection and proper treatment, TB should have no lasting affect on the health of a child.

TREATMENT
In all types of tuberculosis, early diagnosis and treatment is most important. Strict adherence to treatment regimens is essential for both cure of the disease and protection of family and friends.

Modern drug treatment has made it possible to "cure" rather than merely "arrest" tuberculosis in both adults and children. Although a variety of anti-TB drugs now are available (including the promising rifampin, released for clinical use in 1971), physicians say the most useful drug for treating TB in children is isoniazid (INH), administered in combination with one or more of the other drugs, most commonly para-amino-salicylic acid (PAS) or Ethambutol.

In most cases, medication is continued for twelve to eighteen months. Bed rest is infrequently recommended at the onset of treatment.

If hospitalization is indicated, general hospitals near the child's home are used, and usually the period of hospitalization is very brief. Chemotherapy is frequently completely administered on an out-patient basis, however. The child may go to school while continuing drug treatment, once his health is restored and the drugs have rendered his disease noninfectious.

Because modern medicines chemically "isolate" the TB patient, there is no longer need for lengthy confinement in special sanatoriums or hospitals. Climate is no longer considered important in the treatment of TB.

TESTS   After the first infection, the body's cells become sensitized to the particular proteins of the tubercle bacilli. Therefore, when an infected person is given a tuberculin test with a substance containing these proteins, he demonstrates an allergic skin reaction. There are several alternate techniques for the tuberculin test; the one most commonly used is to inject between the layers of skin, usually on the forearm, a small amount of tuberculin.

The test makes no distinction between infected and diseased persons. Other steps must be taken to find out if infected persons have an active case of the disease.

PROGNOSIS   The success of treatment depends greatly on continuing medical supervision. Periodic chest X-rays and sputum examinations plus guidance by a physician are the necessary ingredients. Without close supervision, symptomless patients may discontinue drugs prematurely, thus reducing the chances of recovery.

FUTURE MEDICAL GOALS   Removal of the conditions which lower resistance and make the body more susceptible to tuberculosis infection will help prevent TB. This means improving health standards, especially in areas where hygiene and nutrition are poor. Continuing public education to correct outmoded ideas about tuberculosis and eradicate the stigma still attached to the disease is an essential part of the prevention program.

SERVICES

SPECIALISTS Pediatricians and internists are concerned with the treatment and management of children with tuberculosis. Thoracic specialists, however, are specifically concerned with the treatment of tuberculosis and related diseases.

COMMUNITY HEALTH INFORMATION Information about TB is available from local health departments and from any of the more than 800 state and local Tuberculosis and Respiratory Disease (Christmas Seal) Associations affiliated with the National Tuberculosis and Respiratory Disease Association.

STATE HEALTH PROGRAM Tuberculosis is required by law to be reported to the state departments of health in all states. States vary in services provided to individual patients, but some form of care for indigent TB patients is available in all.

FEDERAL RESEARCH PROGRAM The National Institute of Allergy and Infectious Diseases, Bethesda, Maryland, is concerned with various aspects of tuberculosis immunology.

VOLUNTARY HEALTH ASSOCIATION National Tuberculosis and Respiratory Disease Association
1740 Broadway
New York, N.Y. 10019
The national headquarters is affiliated with fifty constituent associations, consisting of a state association in each of the fifty states and associations in the District of Columbia, Chicago, New York City, Queens, Brooklyn (N.Y.), Guam, Puerto Rico, and the Virgin Islands. Approximately 800 local associations are affiliated with the constituent associations.

HISTORY OF ASSOCIATION
The National Association for the Study and

Prevention of Tuberculosis was the first major voluntary health association in the United States. Founded in 1904, the association was the parent of the organization as we now know it. The name was shortened to National Tuberculosis Association in 1918 and changed to National Tuberculosis and Respiratory Disease Association, reflecting its broadened field of interest in 1968. The founding members formed the association, determined to wage a nationwide campaign against TB— then the leading cause of death in the United States—through the dissemination of information concerning the cause, prevention, and treatment of the disease and through the encouragement of research, preventive procedures, and scientific treatment.

The Association has broadened its interests to include the control of other diseases of the respiratory system, such as such major causes of disability as emphysema and chronic bronchitis, as well as influenza and the common cold; it also sponsors campaigns against cigarette-smoking and air pollution because of their health hazards.

SERVICES OF NATIONAL HEADQUARTERS
Makes referrals to affiliates and makes available literature and films. Its program also includes a nationally administered program of professional education, as well as research and provision of medical information to physicians.

SERVICE OF AFFILIATES
The programs and services of affiliates vary widely and may include: tuberculin testing; cooperating with official health agencies on state and local levels to administer isoniazid to infected individuals living in high-risk areas, who may be exposed to active cases; sponsoring of studies to evaluate the services of tuberculosis clinics, and improvement of laboratory services for the diagnosis and treatment of patients with tuberculosis and other respiratory diseases.

Approximately 200,000 volunteers participate in the activities of state, local, and national associations. All levels of the association are equipped to provide information about TB and other respiratory diseases to concerned citizens.

VOCABULARY

BCG — (for bacillus-Calmette-Guérin) A vaccine used in prevention of TB primarily for children who run a high risk of exposure.

Primary TB — Initial infection seen mostly in children. Usually causes no symptoms in early stages and is indicated by tuberculin skin test.

Venereal Disease

DESCRIPTION OF CONDITION

It is estimated that 600,000 youngsters under twenty were infected with venereal disease last year. The actual figure is impossible to determine because a large percentage of cases are not reported to health authorities. The majority of cases are treated by private practitioners.

The word *venereal* comes from the Latin name Venus, goddess of love. There are five venereal diseases, *chancroid; gonorrhea; granuloma inguinale; lymphogranuloma venereum;* and *syphilis.* The abbreviation VD is used for any or all of them.

Syphilis is caused by a corkscrew-shaped microorganism called a spirochete which can live only in the human body. Syphilis is in effect two diseases: an acute, highly infectious disease spread by contact between individuals; and a chronic disabling one. The chronic form develops in ten to twenty years if the initial infection is not recognized and treated. The disease can produce heart disease, blindness, paralysis, insanity, and possibly death. There is a period just after infection, lasting several months, when the victim may infect others by sexual contact, further spreading the disease. Blindness may occur in an infant born of an infected mother. This is one reason that silver nitrate is placed in the eyes of all newborn.

The venereal disease called gonorrhea is even more widespread than syphilis, especially among younger people. Gonorrhea normally affects only the sex organs, causing a local inflammation. However, if untreated the inflammation may produce changes in the genital tracts of both women and men and may result in sterility. Unlike syphilis, which may give few warning signs, gonorrhea makes its presence known in males by attacking the urinary passage, causing a painful sensation and visible discharge.

TREATMENT

The body reacts against syphilis, but not strongly enough to defeat it. Penicillin, properly used, can control and cure the disease in a person who becomes infected. Prompt treatment is required to prevent the spread of the infection to others. Penicillin treatment is also used to cure gonorrhea and prevent lasting damage to the body.

TESTS In the first few weeks of syphilis, spirochetes from sores can be identified with a phase contrast microscope. In the later stages, the presence of the disease can be proved only by blood tests. The diagnosis is made by finding the organism in serum (fluid) that has been obtained from a sore or from the regional lymph nodes and examined under a microscope.

The gonorrhea test is a simple slide smear test or culture. The attack of the disease upon the female sex organs is complicated, and renders it difficult to diagnose. Nevertheless doctors can determine whether traces of the infection are present.

FUTURE MEDICAL GOALS Future goals include greater effort in VD prevention and control and research toward discovery of a vaccine.

SERVICES

SPECIALISTS A family physician can treat individuals who suspect they have become infected with a venereal disease.

COMMUNITY HEALTH INFORMATION Most city and county health departments maintain special venereal disease clinics. At the majority of these clinics treatment is free. Individuals who are known to have been exposed to infectious venereal disease may be treated as a preventive measure. Some clinics are conducted by private voluntary hospitals.

FEDERAL RESEARCH PROGRAM The National Institutes of Allergy and Infectious Diseases, Bethesda, Maryland, conducts research into venereal disease. A recent workshop explored the gonococcus, an organism causing venereal disease. As a result, a program was undertaken by the Institute to enlarge the knowledge of this organism. Gonorrhea is expected to affect about two million Americans annually in the 1970s.

VOLUNTARY HEALTH ASSOCIATION

American Social Health Association
1740 Broadway
New York, N.Y. 10019

The Association does not have any state or local units. It serves primarily as a resource agency working with and through local organizations which operate permanently in their communities.

HISTORY OF ASSOCIATION

The American Social Health Association was founded in 1912. From the beginning its stated purpose was "to promote those conditions of living, environment, and personal conduct which best protect the family as a social institution." The Association's overall objective is carried out through campaigns against venereal disease, commercialized prostitution, and drug dependence and abuse.

SERVICES OF ASSOCIATION

The Association does not maintain member clinics or treatment centers. It serves primarily as a resource agency working with and through local organizations which operate permanently in their communities.

Literature on venereal disease is available from the Association. Pamphlets may also be ordered in large quantities for groups.

A film, "VD: A Call to Action," may be rented for $20.00 a showing or may be purchased for $300.00. The films are distributed by Association Films, Inc., 866 Third Avenue, New York, N.Y., 10022.

VOCABULARY

Congenital syphilis —That type which is passed from an infected mother while child is in the womb.

Gonococcus —The common name for the organism causing gonorrhea.

Prophylactic treatment —Prevention of a disease by treatment in advance of its appearance.

Reagin —An antibodylike substance in serum and spinal fluid that reacts against syphilis.

STS —Serologic test for syphilis. There are several kinds of tests used.

Part Two
GENERAL INFORMATION

COMMUNITY SERVICES
Local Departments of Health
Community Councils Information Services
Religion-Affiliated Services
Homemaker-Home Health Aides
Visiting Nurse Services
Speech Therapists
Physical Therapists
Services of Medical and Dental Schools/University Services
Fraternal Health Services

STATE SERVICES FOR HANDICAPPED CHILDREN
Description of Crippled Children's Program
State Agencies Administering Services for Handicapped Children
Special Education
Rehabilitation Services

GOVERNMENT SERVICES
National Institutes of Health
Library Services
Tax Deductions

HEALTH PLANS AND INSURANCE INFORMATION
Group Health Insurance Plans
Insurance Information

RECREATION FOR THE HANDICAPPED
Scouts
Summer Camps
Recreational Programs

EMERGENCY SERVICES

Community Services

LOCAL DEPARTMENTS OF HEALTH

The Crippled Children's Services program has been designed to provide medical care in the child's community. The local health department is liaison between the child's family and medical or paramedical services. In most instances it coordinates case-finding, diagnosis, treatment, rehabilitative services, and follow-up care. The local health department and state department of health share legal responsibility for determining financial eligibility for treatment.

Federal law stipulates that any person or agency may refer a child to a Crippled Children's Services program. The largest proportion of case-finding is done by the local health officer and his public health nursing and social work staff through observation of children in schools and public clinics.

Health departments vary from community to community depending upon the wealth of the municipality, the degree of autonomy accorded it by the state government, and the number of people the local department serves. New York City, San Francisco, Baltimore, and a few other major cities have almost complete autonomy; most smaller cities have a directly subordinate position.

The size of the staff of a city health department depends primarily upon the size of the population served. In addition to the health officer, the larger departments may include specialists in public health and preventive medicine who limit their practice to this field. In most municipal health departments the public health nurses constitute approximately one-half of the total staff. Other members of the staff serve the department of health in a part-time capacity, devoting the remainder of their time to private practice. The professional staff may include dentists, chemists, bacteriologists, speech therapists, sanitary engineers, and social workers.

COMMUNITY COUNCILS INFORMATION SERVICES

Prior to 1930, there were no more than twenty-five local Councils in the United States and Canada. Today in close to 500 communities—twenty-seven million families—benefit by child care, family service, youth guidance, health programs, disaster relief, and services for the Armed Forces from 31,000 United Way agencies. All are members of United Community Funds and Councils of America, Inc., and are dedicated to determining, alleviating and preventing social and health problems in the community through organized efforts of local citizens.

About fifty Councils in larger communities maintain referral and information departments. In smaller communities the service is provided by general staff on a part-time basis. Some Councils periodically publish directories of community health and welfare resources in their communities.

Depending on the locality, a Community Council may be called United Good Neighbor Fund, United Community Fund, Welfare Council, Community Chest, United Fund, Inc., Social Planning Council, United Givers, etc.

RELIGION-AFFILIATED SERVICES

Federation of Protestant Welfare Agencies, Federation of Jewish Philanthropies, and Catholic Charities are the largest religion-affiliated federations of institutions and agencies with a network of health and welfare programs. They provide a wide range of direct family, community, youth activities, and youth guidance services.

Adapting themselves to the needs of the communities they serve, agencies may focus their efforts on the problems of drug abuse, old age, and the emotional illness of young adults; in low-income areas Visiting Nurse Services may be extended.

Agencies may also provide vocational guidance to the handicapped, summer camp programs, and diagnostic and psychiatric treatment for disturbed children. Many thousands of sick and injured patients are treated in the affiliated hospitals and institutions.

The religion-affiliated agencies are listed in the telephone book, or community information bureaus of Community Councils know their local affiliates.

HOMEMAKER-HOME HEALTH AIDES

An agency, the National Council for Homemaker Services, Inc., was incorporated in 1962 to stimulate the expansion and improvement of homemaker-home health aide services throughout the United States. Recently, the agency, which is headquartered at 1740 Broadway, New York, N.Y., 10019, changed its name to the National Council for Homemaker-Home Health Aide Services, Inc., to better describe its services which embrace both the health and welfare field.

A homemaker-home health aide is a mature, trained, and professionally supervised woman who is skilled in homemaking, child care, and in the care of the chronically ill and who can help at times of stress. There are about 30,000 aides in the United States and some 2,500 programs. The services of homemaker-home health aides are paid for in a variety of ways: either by direct fees for services or through private insurance programs and public welfare and health services. The local United Fund or community planning council and the public health, welfare or mental health departments are good sources of information about the homemaker services.

VISITING NURSE SERVICES

A visiting nurse is a registered nurse who follows orders given by a doctor and performs the duties of sick care, such as changing surgical dressings, and instructing the family in the use of special equipment in the home of the patient.

Generally, the initial request for nursing services is made by the doctor, who gives information about the diagnosis and specific instructions for treatment and medication. A request for the services of a visiting nurse may be made by the family.

The Visiting Nurse Association is usually a community-based group supported by contributions from local fund-raising organizations. In communities without a Visiting Nurse Association, the local health department often assumes these responsibilities.

There are either no charges or moderate fees, depending on the financial circumstances of the families visited. The address and telephone number of the local Visiting Nurse Association can be found in the telephone directory. If none is listed, the city, county, or state health department or the local United Fund headquarters are sources of information.

SPEECH THERAPISTS Speech problems occur most commonly among children who have cerebral palsy, impaired hearing, cleft lip or palate or who are retarded or brain damaged. However, some children with speech problems have no other disabilities.

Speech therapists, more recently called communications specialists, are trained to understand the complex psychological, physiological, and anatomical factors generally involved in the causes and correction of faulty speech. Local schools, particularly those with classes for the handicapped, and voluntary health associations that serve handicaps most frequently in need of speech therapy, are good sources of information about professional therapists in the community.

The National Association of Hearing and Speech Agencies, 919 18 Street, N.W., Washington, D.C., 20006, was established over fifty years ago with the purpose of promoting high standards of professional service to people with hearing and speech difficulties. Affiliated with the national association are 169 member agencies where a youngster with a hearing or speech difficulty can receive some or all of the following services: diagnosis and evaluation, preschool hearing instruction, counseling and guidance, rehabilitation, and recreational activities. The association makes referrals to member affiliates.

PHYSICAL THERAPISTS Physical therapists work with the medical staffs of hospitals, rehabilitation centers, physicians' offices, and schools for handicapped children and on home-care programs. Physical therapists may also work for the orthopedic specialists or *physiatrists* (rehabilitation specialists). The physical therapist aids in strengthening and restoring function to the patient's muscles, nerves, and joints, and helps to relieve pain and correct deformities.

The licensed physical therapist has completed a four-year college course in physical therapy which includes studies in the biological, physical, and social sciences, followed by training in the use of all the physical modalities for treatment of the sick and disabled. A student is not qualified to practice until he has fulfilled the field experience requirements and has obtained a certificate of proficiency in physical therapy from his college.

Arrangements for physical therapy are made by the patient's physician.

SERVICES OF MEDICAL AND DENTAL SCHOOLS/ UNIVERSITY SERVICES

Medical and dental schools and their affiliated hospital or out-patient departments accept patients. If research is being conducted, only patients with a specific condition are accepted.

For the most part, clinics are used to teach medical and dental students, but treatment of patients is carefully supervised by teaching physicians. Dental clinics provide routine dental care by undergraduates under supervision. Orthodontia and other less routine dental problems are handled by specialists. Fees charged are less than those of a private physician. In some institutions services are free.

Universities often have psychological counseling, speech therapy, and, in some instances, physical therapy and recreational facilities. The community services office of the university can supply information.

FRATERNAL HEALTH SERVICES

The Benevolent and Protective Order of Elks finances programs for youngsters with cerebral palsy in some areas. Physical therapists, speech therapists, and occupational therapists travel in specially equipped station wagons, visiting patients on a regular schedule.

Lions International extends services to some handicapped children and their families by donating ambulances, beds, and other apparatus; sponsors blood banks; encourages preventive and educational health programs. Some Lions Clubs purchase eye-testing equipment, braillewriters, and tape recorders for schools and individuals. They operate summer camps for blind youngsters, and provide recreational centers.

Other fraternal organizations sponsor hospitals, recreational programs, buy equipment, and provide needed services for handicapped children in their area.

The referral and information departments of the community council knows of the health services of fraternal organizations locally.

State Services
for Handicapped Children

HISTORY Tax-supported programs for handicapped children in this country began with the passage of the Social Security Act of 1935.

The Act authorized Congress to appropriate up to $2,850,000 in 1935

for the purpose of enabling each State to extend and improve (particularly in rural areas and those suffering from severe economic distress) as far as practicable in each State, services for locating crippled children and providing medical, surgical, corrective, and other services, as well as care and facilities for diagnosis, hospitalization and after-care, for children who are crippled or suffering from conditions which lead to crippling.

Up to that time most of the services had been confined to efforts by voluntary groups, such as the National Society for the Prevention of Blindness, American Speech and Hearing Association, National Association for Cerebral Palsy, National Society for Crippled Children and Adults.

DESCRIPTION OF SERVICES At first, the state programs, called "The Crippled Children's Program," provided only for children with handicaps needing orthopedic or plastic treatment. This meant that health services were confined mainly to handicaps that could be seen. Through these programs, early diagnosis and treatment of cleft palate, dentofacial handicaps, clubfoot, and congenital malformations combined with surgical advances changed these conditions from chronic to mild or moderate ones. Advances in use of drugs to minimize recurrent attacks of rheumatic fever and the later development of cardiac surgery formed the basis for public programs for rheumatic and congenital heart disease.

Throughout the country, physically handicapped children who are under twenty-one years of age meet the state's requirement of eligibility. Orthopedic or plastic treatment is provided for such handicaps as cleft palate, cleft lips, and clubfeet. Children who have serious burns, accidental injuries, bone deformities, and paralyzed muscles are also eligible for treatment. In addition, the Crippled Children's agencies in all states treat cerebral palsy and congenital heart disease. Nearly all states have facilities for treatment of children with epilepsy, cystic fibrosis, and serious vision and hearing problems. Other conditions that the medical staff of a clinic feel would lead to a crippling condition are also treated.

Frequently local doctors, teachers, and health officials report to the state or local agency that children need attention. A private doctor sometimes requests consultation with specialists at the clinic.

Crippled Children's Program clinics are generally held at regular intervals in permanent locations. In some rural areas, a traveling clinic has been established in order to reach all who need its services. When a clinic travels from place to place, the date and time it will be in a specific area is announced in newspapers or by posters in the post office and local stores. Physicians and local department of health personnel also know where and when the clinics will be held.

Some clinics are treatment clinics for a wide variety of conditions. Others are diagnostic, concerned mainly with determining the particular condition of the child, and making arrangements for treatment. Some clinics, however, combine both diagnostic services and treatment in one facility.

In an attempt to broaden the services of a clinic the state agency may employ specialists on a part-time basis in addition to the regular staff, or the local health department may conduct additional clinics.

Ideally a clinic for handicapped children includes the following professional and paramedical personnel:

Pediatrician—Responsible for obtaining a medical history and giving a child a complete health examination.

Orthopedist—Examines the child for a particular handicap and recommends treatment.

Surgical specialist—Called upon to perform pediatric surgery.

Speech pathologist and audiologist—Examine the child for disorder of speech and hearing and make recommendations.

Dentist—Responsible for preventive services, treatment, correction of defects, and aftercare.

Prosthetist and/or orthotist—Advises the physician on braces and appliances.

Public health nurse—Talks with parents about the health of the child and treatment advised by physician.

Physical therapist—Assists orthopedist and sees that recommendations are carried out in the treatment center or in the home.

Nutritionist—Evaluates adequacy of diet and interprets physician's dietary recommendations for the child in terms of foods that are familiar and available.

Occupational therapist—Plans activities appropriate to child's level; refers parents to recreational facilities in the community.

Medical social worker—Helps parents make particular emotional adjustments; assists in financial problems that must be solved.

ELIGIBILITY The probable cost of complete treatment and rehabilitation for the future, and the effect the financial burden will have on the family, are taken into consideration to determine the eligibility of a patient for handicapped children's services. The state budget is also a consideration, making eligibility slightly different from state to state. Welfare departments set different standards of eligibility for assistance for families with handicapped children where long-term costly care and therapy are needed. A family not entitled to public assistance may be entitled to health services without cost or with a fee based on ability to pay.

Diagnostic services are generally available to all, regardless of economic status, based on the assumption that a diagnosis is usually necessary to estimate the overall cost and duration of treatment. Families who might otherwise be able to afford private medical care frequently consult specialists in clinics sponsored by the program.

For information about complete services and facilities for handicapped children and eligibility, write to the agencies administering services for such children listed here.

STATE AGENCIES ADMINISTERING SERVICES FOR HANDICAPPED CHILDREN

ALABAMA
State Department of Education, Division of Rehabilitation and Crippled Children, State Office Building, Montgomery, Alabama, 36104

ALASKA
State Department of Health and Welfare, Division of Child Health, Pouch "H," Juneau, Alaska, 99801

ARIZONA
State of Arizona Crippled Children's Services, 1825 East Garfield Street, Phoenix, Arizona, 85006

ARKANSAS
State Department of Public Welfare, Crippled Children's Division, State Capitol Mall, Little Rock, Arkansas, 72203

CALIFORNIA
State Department of Public Health, Crippled Children Services, 2151 Berkeley Way, Berkeley, California, 94704

COLORADO
State Department of Health, Crippled Children Section, 4210 East 11th Avenue, Denver, Colorado, 80220

CONNECTICUT	State Department of Health, Crippled Children's Services, 79 Elm Street, Hartford, Connecticut, 06115
DELAWARE	State Board of Health, Crippled Children's Services, State Health Building, Dover, Delaware, 19901
DISTRICT OF COLUMBIA	Department of Public Health, Bureau of Maternal and Child Health, 1875 Connecticut Avenue, Washington, D.C., 20001
FLORIDA	Crippled Children's Commission, 107 West Gaines Street, Tallahassee, Florida, 32304
GEORGIA	State Department of Public Health, Crippled Children's Services, 47 Trinity Avenue S.W., Atlanta, Georgia, 30303
GUAM	Department of Public Health and Social Services, Crippled Children's Services, Territory of Guam, P.O. Box 2816, Agana, Guam, 96910
HAWAII	State Department of Health, Crippled Children Branch, P.O. Box 3378, Honolulu, Hawaii, 96801
IDAHO	State Department of Health, Crippled Children's Service, 509 North 5th St., Room 210, Boise, Idaho, 83701
ILLINOIS	University of Illinois, Division of Services for Crippled Children, 540 Iles Park Place, Springfield, Illinois, 62703
INDIANA	State Department of Public Welfare, Services for Crippled Children, 100 North Senate Avenue, Indianapolis, Indiana, 46204
IOWA	The University of Iowa, State Services for Crippled Children, 500 Newton Road, Iowa City, Iowa, 52241
KANSAS	Crippled Children's Commission, 727 First National Bank Building, Wichita, Kansas, 67202
KENTUCKY	Commission for Handicapped Children, 1405 East Burnett Avenue, Louisville, Kentucky, 40217
LOUISIANA	State Department of Health, Crippled Children's Services, Civic Center, P.O. Box 60630, New Orleans, Louisiana, 70160
MAINE	State Department of Health and Welfare, Division of Child Health, State House, Augusta, Maine, 04330
MARYLAND	State Department of Health, Crippled Children's Services, State Office Building, 301 West Preston Street, Baltimore, Maryland, 21201

MASSACHUSETTS	State Department of Public Health, Division of Maternal and Child Health, Clinics for Crippled Children, Boston, Massachusetts, 02133
MICHIGAN	State Department of Public Health, Services to Crippled Children, Lansing, Michigan, 48913
MINNESOTA	Department of Public Welfare, Crippled Children's Services, Centennial Building, St. Paul, Minnesota, 55101
MISSISSIPPI	State Department of Education, Crippled Children's Services, Jackson, Mississippi, 39206
MISSOURI	University of Missouri, Crippled Children's Service, Columbia, Missouri, 65201
MONTANA	State Department of Health, Child Health Services Division, Crippled Children, Helena, Montana, 59601
NEBRASKA	State Department of Public Welfare, Services for Crippled Children, Capitol Building, Lincoln, Nebraska, 68509
NEVADA	Department of Health, Welfare, and Rehabilitation, Crippled Children's Services, 201 South Fall Street, Carson City, Nevada, 89701
NEW HAMPSHIRE	State Department of Health and Welfare, Crippled Children's Services, State Health Building, 61 South Spring Street, Concord, New Hampshire, 03301
NEW JERSEY	State Department of Health, Crippled Children Service, P.O. Box 1540, Trenton, New Jersey, 08625
NEW MEXICO	State Department, Health and Social Services Department, Crippled Children's Services Unit, P.O. Box 2348, Sante Fe, New Mexico, 87501
NEW YORK	State Department of Health, Bureau of Medical Rehabilitation, 28 Essex Street, Albany, New York, 12208
NORTH CAROLINA	State Board of Health, Crippled Children's Services, 225 North McDowell Street, Raleigh, North Carolina, 27602
NORTH DAKOTA	Public Welfare Board of North Dakota, Crippled Children's Services, Bismarck, North Dakota, 58501
OHIO	State Department of Public Welfare, Crippled Children's Services, 408 East Town Street, Columbus, Ohio, 43215

OKLAHOMA	Department of Institutions, Social and Rehabilitative Services, Crippled Children's Unit, Oklahoma City, Oklahoma, 73105
OREGON	University of Oregon Medical School, Crippled Children's Division, 3181 Southwest Sam Jackson Park Road, Portland, Oregon, 97201
PENNSYLVANIA	State Department of Health, Division of Maternal and Child Health, Crippled Children's Services, Harrisburg, Pennsylvania, 17120
PUERTO RICO	Insular Department of Health, Crippled Children Services, Ponce de Leon Avenue, San Juan, Puerto Rico, 00908
RHODE ISLAND	State Department of Health, Crippled Children's Division, Providence, Rhode Island, 02903
SOUTH CAROLINA	State Department of Health, Crippled Children's Services, J. Marion Sims Building, Columbia, South Carolina, 29201
SOUTH DAKOTA	State Department of Health, Crippled Children's Services, Pierre, South Dakota, 57501
TENNESSEE	State Department of Public Health, Crippled Children's Services, Nashville, Tennessee, 37219
TEXAS	State Department of Health, Crippled Children's Service, 1100 West 49th Street, Austin, Texas, 78756
UTAH	State Department of Health and Welfare, Crippled Children's Services, Salt Lake City, Utah, 84111
VERMONT	State Department of Health, Division of Handicapped Children's Services, Burlington, Vermont, 05401
VIRGINIA	State Department of Health, Bureau of Crippled Children's Services, Richmond, Virginia, 23219
VIRGIN ISLANDS	Insular Department of Health, Services for Crippled Children, Charlotte Amalie, St. Thomas, Virgin Islands, 00802
WASHINGTON	State Department of Health, Crippled Children's Services, Olympia, Washington, 98502
WEST VIRGINIA	Department of Welfare, Division of Crippled Children's Services, Charleston, West Virginia, 25305
WISCONSIN	State Department of Public Instruction, Bureau of Handicapped Children, Madison, Wisconsin, 53702

WYOMING State Department of Public Health, Division of Maternal and Child Health and Crippled Children, Cheyenne, Wyoming, 82001

SPECIAL EDUCATION It is estimated that only about one-fourth of the handicapped children in the United States who require special education are being served by special school programs, and there are only about one-fourth as many special teachers as are needed. Some programs, however, are outstanding.

For information about education of handicapped children ask the local Board of Education what the public schools provide. Large cities have a department of Special Education that is responsible for the schooling of physically and mentally handicapped children.

If the public school system does not provide the right school situation, there may be a private school established or sponsored by some nongovernmental organizations interested in the handicapped, such as the United Cerebral Palsy Associations, chapters of the National Association for Retarded Children, and the National Society for Crippled Children and Adults.

Often a local family agency or Council of Social Agencies will have information about the facilities of public, private and residential schools for the handicapped.

Porter Sargent's *Directory for Exceptional Children*, available in many libraries, lists some 2,000 programs for training and education of exceptional children, including more than 1,000 clinics. The Council for Exceptional Children, a Department of the National Education Association, 1201 16th Street, N.W., Washington, D.C., is a source of publications and information about handicapped children's education.

REHABILITATION/ VOCATIONAL COUNSELING The nationwide federal-state system of vocational rehabilitation operates through ninety-one agencies. These include a general agency serving persons with any type of disability in each of the fifty states, the District of Columbia, Puerto

Rico, Guam, and the Virgin Islands, as well as an agency in thirty-seven states serving only the blind. All these agencies have the responsibility of providing vocational rehabilitation services to the handicapped.

The aim of the state rehabilitation agencies is to prepare a disabled person for employment, then to secure his placement in a job which best utilizes his physical and mental capacities. The services include counseling, physical restoration, training, and placement with follow-up. In addition, some state agencies provide auxiliary services which include transportation and also help supply disabled persons with necessary tools, equipment, and licenses. The state agencies cooperate extensively with other public and voluntary agencies interested in working with the disabled.

The best source of information is the State Office of Vocational Rehabilitation. Each state has such an office, and most states have several in different communities. These are usually listed in the telephone book. The local, county, or state health department, a family service agency, the council of social agencies, or the local and state department of education can also be referred to for information on vocational counseling programs for the handicapped.

Government Services

NATIONAL INSTITUTES OF HEALTH

GOVERNMENT HEALTH SERVICES

The National Institutes of Health (NIH), an agency of the Department of Health, Education, and Welfare, is concerned with improving the health of people. The Institutes are located in a series of buildings on a 300-acre "campus" at Bethesda, Maryland, and are concerned with the following:

Research to learn more about what causes disease and new ways to overcome it; provision to nonprofit institutions of facilities for research and medical education, such as buildings, animals, equipment, and library services; training of men and women to carry on research; education of physicians and allied health professionals to bring the results of research into practice.

The Institutes are not, however, directly involved in health services, and only admit for treatment those patients who are referred to them by their physicians to participate in a particular research effort currently underway at NIH.

The Institutes maintain hundreds of laboratories, a 516-bed clinical research facility, and the National Library of Medicine with over a million volumes. The National Institutes of Health also serve to administer Federal funds in support of efforts by nonprofit research and teaching institutions in the field of health. Over three-fourths of the NIH funds are appropriated to support these nationwide activities by individual research grants, fellowships, and training grants to scientists and researchers in universities, medical schools, hospitals, and clinics.

Grants are also awarded to help in construction or renovation of laboratories for special research resources, and to fund the costs of special equipment to be used by scientists within an entire region.

The National Institutes of Health have responsibility for the safety, purity, and potency of all vaccines, blood, serums, antitoxins, and other biological products sold in interstate commerce or exported. They set standards for these and license the products and the manufacturers.

NATIONAL CANCER INSTITUTE
The National Cancer Institute conducts research relating to the cause, prevention, and methods of diagnosis and treatment of cancer. Cancer research is also conducted through research grants to institutions such as universities, medical schools, and hospitals. Research training grants are available to qualified institutions, and postdoctoral and special fellowships to qualified individuals

In recent research on cause and prevention, emphasis has been given to promising work on viruses in relation to human cancer. In treatment, since curative surgery and radiation are limited to essentially localized conditions, scientists continue to develop new drugs for systemic or disseminated cancer and improve the techniques for using them. Fundamental research in molecular biology has concentrated largely on the chemistry of life at the subcellular level. A scientist working under a National Cancer Institute grant reported the first complete synthesis of a gene.

The National Cancer Institute appropriation for grants and direct operations in the year 1950 was $18,900,000; the appropriation for fiscal year 1972 was $337,500,000.

NATIONAL EYE INSTITUTE
The National Eye Institute became an independent organization within the National Institutes of Health during 1970. This autonomous status was attained with the transfer of vision programs from the National Institute of Neurological Diseases and Stroke.

The mission of the National Eye Institute is to support and conduct research into the causes, natural history, prevention, diagnosis, and treatment of disorders of the eye and visual system and in related fields.

It was through NIH supported research that the blinding condition in newborn infants known as retrolental fibroplasia was virtually eliminated in the early 1950s, with the discovery of oxygen overuse as the cause. Recently, however, for premature infants high oxygen therapy has been found successful in saving the lives of those who develop hypoxia or respiratory distress. In these cases (some 40,000 a year) there is a need for constant ophthalmic monitoring. The Institute is concerned with improving existing methods of monitoring.

Research is also being conducted into: use of the argon gas laser as a new tool for treating visual disorders not responsive to other forms of therapy; medical management of cataracts; prevention and treatment of congenital eye defects, amblyopia, and refractive errors; and the process by which the informational content of light, determined by its image on the retina, is converted into meaningful symbols for the brain.

NATIONAL HEART AND LUNG INSTITUTE

In 1969 the National Heart Institute was renamed the National Heart and Lung Institute and given the primary responsibility for federally supported research into emphysema and other chronic lung diseases. These diseases are beginning to rival coronary heart disease as a cause of disability, and the death toll of patients suffering from them has risen alarmingly in recent years.

Key research areas of the Institute include: arteriosclerosis (including coronary and cerebrovascular disease); cardiac diseases (including congenital and rheumatic heart disease); hypertension and kidney disorders; chronic lung disease; thrombosis and hemorrhagic diseases; and cardiac replacement, including transplantation and artificial-heart development. In addition, the Institute conducts a broad program of basic research on the structure, function, metabolism, performance, and regulation of the cardiovascular and pulmonary systems.

NATIONAL INSTITUTE OF ARTHRITIS AND METABOLIC DISEASES
The National Institute of Arthritis and Metabolic Diseases is concerned with the causes, prevention, diagnosis, and treatment of the various arthritic, rheumatic, and collagen diseases; the broad spectrum of metabolic diseases (such as diabetes) and other inborn errors of metabolism; gastroenterology; orthopedics; dermatology; urology and renal disease; mineral metabolism; and subjects related to the above.

The Institute conducts, fosters, and coordinates research in biochemistry; nutrition; pathology; histochemistry; chemistry; physical, chemical, and molecular biology; pharmacology; and toxicology. The Institute has achieved the laboratory synthesis of a new hormone important in regulating the pituitary gland; and is continuing research into the causes of rheumatoid arthritis which implicate viruses or a disorder of the immune system or a combination of both; the role of insulin both in health and in diabetes; and the causes of cystic fibrosis.

The Institute is concerned with kidney diseases and the development of artificial kidneys. New and improved prototypes of artificial kidneys are undergoing experimental work.

NATIONAL INSTITUTE OF ALLERGY AND INFECTIOUS DISEASES
The Institute conducts and coordinates basic research on human diseases caused by infectious organisms and by allergic responses. In 1969, the Institute completed work of successful rubella vaccine field trials and subsequent licensing of a vaccine for commercial use. They have conducted significant research in the field of immunology on the relationship between disease susceptibility and an individual's "histocompatibility profile"—the array of antigens, or foreign substances, which characterize white cells and which are used to "match" tissues in transplantation. Contracts have also been awarded by the Insti-

tute for studies of more efficient methods of assaying, purifying, and producing "interferon," a natural antiviral substance of the body.

NATIONAL INSTITUTE OF CHILD HEALTH AND HUMAN DEVELOPMENT The National Institute of Child Health and Human Development conducts and supports research in human development from the period of conception through old age.

Within the framework of research on population, early childhood development and the related areas of nutrition and mental retardation, the Institute has investigated the following: medical effects of existing methods of fertility control and the social and behavioral aspects of population change; the effects of malnutrition on critical developmental stages in animals; studies of human populations suffering from severe malnutrition; the development of reading ability through training of infants and very young children with visual and auditory stimulation.

NATIONAL INSTITUTE OF DENTAL RESEARCH The National Institute of Dental Research conducts, fosters, and coordinates research into the causes, prevention, diagnosis, and treatment of oral and dental diseases and conditions.

Recently preliminary tests conducted by the Institute have shown that treatment with a plastic sealant can prevent for two years the most common form of tooth decay, which begins in small pits and grooves on the biting surfaces of children's teeth. This colorless adhesive seems quick, safe, painless, and easy to paint on the chewing surfaces of clean, slightly etched teeth. It is now being tested on a large scale to learn whether it fulfills its promise.

To attract scientists in disciplines formerly not involved in dental research, the National Institute of Dental Research supports research at several universities to contribute new knowledge and provide stimulating environments for training researchers and teachers. The Institute has prepared a *Directory of U.S. Facilities Providing Cleft Lip and Cleft Palate Services*. In connection with cleft palate studies, an Institute scientist has adapted an instrument called a lock-in amplifier to detect deafness in animals and children. The test can even be done on a sleeping infant. Early detection of deafness is vital to the process of learning to speak.

Through Institute research a new instrument was devised to measure directly and record the motions of the soft palate without interfering with its functioning, and this may be an important aid in developing control of the palate in speech.

NATIONAL INSTITUTE OF NEUROLOGICAL DISEASES AND STROKE The Institute coordinates research into the causes, prevention, diagnosis, and treatment of neurological, sensory, and communicative disorders. During its history the Institute has developed extensive research programs on all principal neurological and sensory disorders.

The development of L-Dopa, a new drug beneficial to patients with Parkinson's disease, was supported by the Institute. Similarly, research yielded the following: the identification of the missing enzyme in six of the so-called lipid storage disorders, including Tay-Sachs disease; and additional evidence that crippling sclerosing disorders such as multiple sclerosis may be of viral origin. Because at least one in every ten Americans (twenty million) has a communication problem, the Institute is also concerned with studying the field of human communication: hearing, language, and speech.

NATIONAL INSTITUTE OF ENVIRONMENTAL HEALTH SCIENCES The Institute is concerned with the growing Federal responsibility for environmental quality. Their mission is to identify the chemical, physical, and biological factors in the environment that can adversely affect man; to contribute to an understanding of the mechanisms and manifestations of human diseases produced by these agents, and to provide the scientific basis for the development of control measures by other agencies.

DIVISION OF BIOLOGICS STANDARDS

The Division of Biologics Standards is responsible for administering Federal regulations for biologic products for human use; establishing and maintaining the highest possible level of testing and inspection of production facilities for biologic products offered for sale in interstate commerce or for export and import.

NATIONAL INSTITUTE OF GENERAL MEDICAL SCIENCES

The Institute gives priority to four special programs: research in genetic sciences to prevent and alleviate human hereditary diseases; knowledge needed for safer, more effective use of drugs; faster, more reliable, less costly methods and systems for prevention and diagnosis of disease; new and improved ways to care for injured patients in an effort to reduce the death toll in disability caused by trauma.

NATIONAL LIBRARY OF MEDICINE

The Library collects, organizes, and makes available biomedical information to researchers, educators, and practitioners. The Library has a Congressional mandate to apply its resources broadly to the advancement of the medical and health-related sciences.

CLINICAL CENTER

The Clinical Center, research hospital of National Institutes of Health, provides patient care in support of the clinical investigations conducted by ten of the Institutes.

DIVISION OF RESEARCH SERVICES

The Division of Research Services provides the National Institutes of Health with centralized research services including instrumentation development, fabrication, and maintenance; animal production and care; environmental health and sanitation control; medical arts and photography; and the NIH Library and translating services.

NATIONAL INSTITUTE OF MENTAL HEALTH

The National Institute of Mental Health is part of the Health Services and Mental Health Administration of Public Health Service. It administers the Federal Government's major program of support for mental health through research, training, and services. The Institute conducts and supports research into the causes, treatment, and prevention of mental and emotional illnesses and the public health problems related to mental health, such as drug abuse and alcoholism.

Most of the national investment in mental health goes to the states and to state institutions and agencies, to universities, hospitals, and local mental health programs, and to individuals whose work or study is supported by grants. The annual expenditure of the fifty states totals more than $1.5 billion.

One-fourth of the Institute's research budget is spent on the mental health of the young. The Center of Studies of Child and Family Mental Health coordinates a massive program of research and training across the country with particular emphasis on mental health and mental illness in the formative years, on the early treatment of illness, and on its prevention.

The Institute's program in child and family mental health ranges from research in the behavioral and biological sciences to the influences of family and social systems on the young. The national mental health program is a partnership among federal, state, and local governments and private agencies and citizens who provide care for the mentally ill and preventive services to promote people's mental health.

LIBRARY SERVICES

The Library of Congress receives federal funds to maintain a library for the blind and those with visual-perceptual disorders and with physical disabilities where muscle or nerve deterioration or paralysis causes inability to hold a book, turn pages, or focus on print materials. Examples of physical disabilities where these conditions may be present are cerebral palsy, multiple sclerosis, muscular dystrophy, arthritis, poliomyelitis, and diplegia.

Some of the services available are large-print

literature, a music library, and books in braille, talking records and tapes. A system of forty-eight cooperating regional libraries serve as distribution centers for these materials, which are mailed free of charge. Inquiries should be addressed to Division for the Blind and Physically Handicapped, Library of Congress, Washington, D.C., 20542. Local libraries can also give information on services.

TAX DEDUCTIONS

Transportation to visit a physician, including the tolls and parking fees; tuition for a boarding school for a handicapped child, or for a special day school; drugs; medical expenses; and insurance premiums that cover medical care: these are some of the items to which tax deductions may be applied. Where there are major medical expenditures, professional tax advice is particularly important.

Health Plans
and Insurance Information

GROUP HEALTH
PLANS

Some community organizations, labor unions, and consumer cooperatives have contracted with established doctors, groups, or sponsored the establishment of new groups to provide comprehensive health care on a prepaid or budget basis.

The consumer-sponsored plans are different from private medical groups in that subscribers *pay in advance for health services.* These plans differ from Blue Shield, insurance, and other prepayment plans which pay for medical care on a fee-for-service basis and simply reimburse the patient or pay the doctor.

There are about 200 consumer-oriented groups in the United States and Canada, three of them with more than 800,000 members each.

Health Insurance Plan of Greater New York (HIP) is an example of this type of plan. As a nonprofit group, HIP functions as an insurance company that obtains subscribers from employee groups of ten or more people. Its income comes entirely from fixed annual premiums paid jointly by the subscriber and his employer. The insured persons are entitled to any needed medical care carried out at home, in a physician's office, or in a general hospital.

Subscribers choose physicians from those who are members of the plan; they have been carefully selected and checked by the parent organization to insure the quality of professional services. The plan offers comprehensive medical care at a relatively low cost. HIP recently requested a forty-four percent increase in rates because of increased costs; however, patients pay as much as thirty percent less for all medical expenses than those who are not members.

Group Health Association of America, Inc. (GHAA), is a nonprofit organization formed in 1959 to work for the creation and expansion of prepayment group health plans. The association, located at Suite 203, 1717 Massachusetts Avenue N.W., Washington, D.C. 20036, has literature and information of consumer-oriented groups in communities where they exist.

INSURANCE INFORMATION

A large share of private health insurance in the United States is provided by life insurance companies. This protection helps to pay hospital, surgical, and other medical expenses. A central source of information of companies that would consider insuring a handicapped person is the Health Insurance Institute, 277 Park Avenue, New York, 10017.

Recreation for the Handicapped

SCOUTS
In 1917, five years after the first Girl Scout troop was organized, some girls in a home for physically handicapped children decided that they, too, wanted to be Girl Scouts. The establishment and success of this troop paved the way for the organization of other troops of handicapped children in residential schools, hospitals, and at home.

In time, specialists working with handicapped children pointed out the importance of including these children in groups with nonhandicapped youngsters. As a result, more physically disabled members now belong to troops with nonhandicapped girls than to troops made up entirely of handicapped girls.

There are many Girl Scouts with visual and hearing impairments, orthopedic problems and cerebral palsy, cardiac problems, diabetes, epilepsy, and mental retardation.

A small number of troops are made up of girls who are emotionally disturbed or socially maladjusted. These troops are primarily affiliated with hospitals, treatment centers, or training schools.

The Boy Scouts of America welcomes handicapped boys, and works closely with organizations for the handicapped. Like the Girl Scouts, the Boy Scouts try to integrate handicapped boys in troops with the nonhandicapped.

Most local council addresses and telephone numbers are listed in the various telephone directories of the area served. Local affiliates of the voluntary health associations listed under each handicap can also be consulted about the recreational resources in their communities.

SUMMER CAMPS
Scouts do not have special camps for handicapped youngsters. Therefore, whenever possible, the handicapped attend day and residential camps with nonhandicapped Scouts. Several voluntary

health associations sponsor camps for the category they serve. These are indicated under each handicap.

Ys welcome handicapped children to their day and resident camps where it is feasible. Fraternal organizations such as the Rotary have a number of summer camps mainly for physically disabled children. Local Rotary chapters have a list of their locations and restrictions.

RECREATIONAL PROGRAMS Local affiliates of the voluntary health associations, such as the United Cerebral Palsy, Easter Seal Society, and National Society for Autistic Children, have created recreational programs. Some programs are restricted to the handicap the association serves, but others accept all children.

Local Parks Departments, Ys, and community centers often have programs or will consider starting programs of arts and crafts or recreation if interest is expressed.

Emergency Services

AMBULANCE
Call the police emergency number or OPERATOR for an ambulance. Simply give the address or location where the ambulance is needed.

DENTAL EMERGENCIES
For dental emergencies at night, on holidays, or on weekends *only when your own dentist cannot be reached,* dental societies may be consulted.

DOCTORS' EMERGENCY SERVICES
To get a doctor in an emergency, in the event you cannot reach your own doctor, the county medical society will be of help. Most medical societies have physicians they can contact in an emergency. Be sure to give address or location.

POISON
If a youngster has swallowed poison, immediately call your doctor, the department of health, or the nearest Poison Control Center.

PRESCRIPTION EMERGENCY SERVICE
The police has a list of the drugstores open. In an emergency, police will provide whatever transportation may be necessary to expedite delivery of a prescription.

MEDICAL IDENTIFICATION
The Medic Alert Foundation International, 1000 North Palm, Turlock, California, 95380, is the largest organization providing a complete system of emergency data for its members. They maintain a computerized file on each member, listing any hidden or special medical condition, the names of the member's physicians and nearest relative and other pertinent information. A member receives a medallion or bracelet engraved with his medical problems, the member's identification number, the Medic Alert telephone number, and a wallet card.

The Medic Alert emblems are usually worn by diabetics, hemophiliacs, epileptics; persons with myasthenia gravis, multiple sclerosis, severe allergies to beestings, antibiotics, or horse serum; persons taking anticoagulants, cortisone, or other medication. For children who find it particularly difficult to communicate during an emergency a medical identification is invaluable.

Twenty-four-hour telephone service is maintained that accepts collect calls from doctors and other emergency personnel anywhere in the world. The telephone number is 209-634-4917. Medic Alert carries on an active program to educate authorized personnel to look for its emblem.

The American Medical Association and the World Medical Assembly have adopted a universal symbol to alert anyone giving emergency care to a person who is unconscious, or otherwise unable to communicate, that its wearer has a medical condition requiring special attention.

The American Medical Association, 535 North Dearborn Street, Chicago, Illinois, 60610, will send an emergency medical identification card listing the minimum amount of medical information necessary to carry at all times.

Index

Adrenalin, 110
Air pollution dangers, 6
Allergens, 5, 8, 13
Allergies, 3-13, 63, 201-202
  asthma, 8-9
  description of, 3-4
  desensitization injections, 4-5
  drug therapy, 6-7
  educational programs, 12
  immunotherapy, 6, 16-17
  medical progress, 5-6
  services available, 10-13, 201-202
  tests, 7
  treatment, 3-5
Allergists, 10-11
Allergoid, 4-5, 13
Allergy Foundation of America, 10-12
Amblyopia, 40, 200
Ambulances, emergency service, 211
American Academy of Allergy, 11
American Annals of the Deaf, 72
American Association of Workers for
  the Blind, 37
American Association on Mental
  Deficiency, 156
American Blood Bank Association, 61
American Cancer Society, 44-47, 50
  local affiliates, 45-46
  services, 46-47
American College of Allergists, 11
American Dental Association, 80-81
American Diabetes Association, 86-87
American Foundation for the Blind,
  37-38
American Heart Association, 108-110
  services of affiliates, 108-109
American Medical Association, 130, 212
American Organization for the
  Education of the Hearing Impaired, 74
American Red Cross, 61
American Social Health Association,
  91-92, 179
Amniocentesis, 22, 24, 170
Amphetamines, 91, 160-161
Andersen, Dr. Dorothy, 63
Anemia, 44
  Cooley's, 59-62
  hemolytic, 52
  sickle-cell, 165-168
Angiocardiography, 106
Ankylosing spondylitis, 14

Anoxia, 53, 70, 124, 163
Antibiotics, 16, 64-65, 117, 166
Antibodies, 3, 5, 13
Anticonvulsant drugs, 56, 160
Anti-hemophilic factor, 115
Antihistamines, 6, 13
Aorta, 110
Aortic stenosis, 110
Aphasia, development, 124
Aplastic crisis, 168
Arrhythmias, 110
Arthritis and rheumatic diseases, 14-20,
  67
  description of, 14-15
  drug therapy, 16
  education and recreation, 19
  hemophilic arthropathy, 116
  juvenile rheumatoid arthritis, 14-20
  prognosis, 15-16
  services, 17-19
  treatment, 15-16
Arthritis Foundation, 18-19, 26
Artificial kidney machines, 119, 122
Aspirin, 4, 14, 16
Association for Children with Learning
  Disabilities, 128-129
Asthma, 4, 8-9, 63
  description of, 8
  prognosis, 9
Ataxic, 53, 58
Athetoid, 53, 58
Atopy, inherited predisposition, 4
Audiologists, 136, 191
Autism, 131, 135-139
  description of, 135-139
  educational programs, 134
  prognosis, 136
  recreational programs, 137-138
  services, 136-139
  (*See also* Mental illness)
Autoimmune disturbances, 52

Banting, Dr. Frederick G., 84
Barbiturates, 90
Beers, Clifford W., 133
Behavioral problems
  blind and partially sighted, 32
  brain-damaged children, 125-126
Bell, Alexander Graham, Association
  for the Deaf, Inc., 74-75

Best, Charles H., 84
Biochemists, 60, 136, 151, 170
Biologists, 60, 151, 170
Biopsy tests, 44, 149
Birth defects, 21-29
  description of, 21
  inborn errors of metabolic processes,
    24, 29
  medical progress, 23-24
  services, 24-27
    community health information, 24, 29
    Easter Seal Society, 27
    National Foundation-March of
      Dimes, 25-27
  tests, 24
  treatment, 22-23
    genetic counseling, 22, 27-28
    rubella vaccine, 21-22
Birthmarks, 155
"Bleeder's disease," 111
Blindness, 30-41
  behavioral problems, 32
  congenital, 21, 25
  description of, 30-32, 177
  educational programs, 31-32
  financial assistance for parents, 33
  library materials for, 33, 40, 205-206
  ophthalmia neonatorum, 30, 39
  partial sightedness, 30-32
  rehabilitation services, 31-33
  retrolental fibroplasia, 31, 200
  services, 32-40
    list of federal-state programs, 33-37
    voluntary associations, 37-40
  silver nitrate for newborns, 30, 39, 177
  tests, 41
Blood credit programs, 61
Blood pressure
  acute kidney failure, 119
  portal and pulmonary hypertension, 69
Blood tests, 105
  diabetes, 85
  kidney disease, 120
  leukemia, 50
Blood transfusions
  Cooley's anemia, 59-60
  for hemophilia, 111
  for sickle-cell anemia, 165
Blood urea nitrogen (BUN) tests, 120
Blood vessels, diseases of, 4
"Blue babies," 103-104, 110
Blue Shield, 207
Bone diseases, 43, 155
  bone marrow abnormalities, 59, 168
Bow legs, 155
Boy Scout programs for handicapped,
  58, 138, 209
Brain damage, 32, 55, 70, 124
  behavior problems, 125-126

cerebral palsy and, 53
description of, 124-126
drug therapy, 56
educational programs for, 126-127
neurological symptoms, 125
perceptual difficulties, 125-126
perseveration, 126
services, 128-129
tests, 127-128
Brain tumors, 43
Bronchitis, 63
Broncho-dilators, 65
Burns and complications of, 155

Camps and camping, 87, 138, 209-210
Cancer, 42-48
  biopsy tests, 44, 149
  description of, 42-43
  leukemia, 42, 44, 48-52
    (See also Leukemia)
  medical progress, 43-44
  services, 44-45
    volunteer health associations, 45-47
  treatment, 42
  surgery and radiation, 43
Cancer Care, Inc., 45, 47
Capillary walls, 85
Carbohydrates, 87
Carcinogenic substances, 42, 47
Cardiologists, 66, 105, 106
Cartilage, 19-20
Cataracts, 200
Catatonia, 135
Catheterization, cardiac, 105
Catholic Charities, 184-185
Celiac disease, 63, 136
Cerebral palsy, 53-58
  description of, 53
  drug therapy, 56
  educational programs, 54, 58
  medical progress, 55
  prognosis, 54-55
  recreational programs, 58, 210
  services, 56-58, 187-188
  tests, 55-56
  treatment, 54, 56
Chemotherapists, 44
Chemotherapy, 43, 47
Chlorpromazine, 131
Cholesterol, 120
Christmas Seals Society, 174
Chromosomal abnormalities, 22, 159
Cleft palate and lip, 21, 202-203
Clotting factor concentrates, 111-112
Clotting time tests, 113
Clubfoot, 21, 24
Coagulation deficiency, 113
Cobalt treatment, 43, 47

Collagen diseases, 67, 154
Communicative disorders, 72
Community Chest, 184
Community service, 183-188
  community councils information
    services, 184
  fraternal organizations, 187-188
  homemaker-home health aides, 185
  local departments of health, 183
  physical therapists, 186-187
  religion affiliated services, 184-185
  services of medical and dental schools, 187
  speech therapists, 186
  visiting nurse services, 184-186
Congenital anomalies, 21, 23-25, 27-28
  heart disease, 21, 102-105
Convulsions, 94-96
Cooley's anemia, 59-62
  description of, 59
  medical progress, 60
  services, 60-62
  treatment, 59-60
Cooley's Anemia Blood and Research
  Foundation for Children, 60-61
Cor pulmonale, 69
Cornea, 40
Cortisone, 6
Council for Exceptional Children, 196
CPK serum enzyme determination, 150
Creatine, 150, 154
Crippled Children's Programs (see
  State services)
Cyanosis, 102
Cystic fibrosis, 21, 63-69
  description of, 63, 65-66
  drug therapy, 65
  educational programs, 69
  lung damage, 64, 66
  recreational programs, 69
  services, 66-69
  symptoms, 63
  tests, 65-66
  treatment, 63-65
Cystic Fibrosis Centers, 66-67

Deafness, 70-77
  community health information, 72
  conductive hearing loss, 70, 77
  congenital, 21, 25
  description of, 70
  educational programs, 71-74
    oralist method, 71-72, 74
  hearing aids, 70-72
  prevention in infants, 70
  sensorineural hearing loss, 70-71
  services, 72-76
  tests for, 70-71, 203
  treatment, 70-71

Decibels, 77
Dental problems, 78-79
  community health information, 80
  dental caries, 78, 81
  description of, 78-79
  emergencies, 211
  fluoridation, 79, 82
  malocclusion, 78
  periodontal diseases, 78
  prevention of, 78-79
  services available, 80-81, 187, 202-203
  tests, 79
  treatment, 79, 187
Dentine, definition, 82
Dentists, 54, 56, 78, 191
de Villiers, Robert Roessler, Foundation, 57
Diabetes, 21, 22, 25, 83-88
  community health information, 86
  description of, 83-84
  ketoacidosis and coma, 83
  medical progress, 84-85
  mellitus, 87
  recreational activities, 87
  services available, 86-87
  symptoms, 83-84
  tests, 85
Dialysis, peritoneal, 119
Digestive disorders, 4, 21, 64
  cystic fibrosis, 63
Dilantin, 95
Diphtheria, 4-5
Directory for Exceptional Children
  (Sargent), 196
Diuretics, 123
Division of Biologic Standards, 204
Division of Narcotics Addiction and
  Drug Abuse, 91
DNA (deoxyribonucleic acid), 149
Down's syndrome (mongolism), 28
Drug addiction, 89-92
  community health information, 91
  description of, 89-90
  drug dependence, 89, 92
  habituation, 92
  services, 90-92
  treatment, 90
    rehabilitation facilities, 89
    self-help programs, 90
  withdrawal sickness, 89, 92
Drug therapy
  cerebral palsy, 56
  cystic fibrosis, 65
  epilepsy, 94-96
  heart disease, 103-105
  mental illness, 131-132
  retardation, 160-161
Dyslexia, 124, 129
Dystrophy, 154
  (See also Muscular dystrophy)

Ear diseases, 4
Easter Seal Society, 17, 72, 210
Eczema, 3–4
Educational programs
  arthritis and rheumatic diseases, 19
  blind and partially sighted, 31–32
  brain-damaged children, 126–127
  cerebral palsy patients, 54, 58
  deaf children, 71
  epilepsy, 98–100
  heart disease, 109–110
  mental illness, 134
  muscular dystrophy, 154
  retardation, 156–160
    preschool programs, 156–158
  state sponsored, 196–197
Ego, definition, 135
Electrocardiography (ECG), 105
Electroencephalography (EEG), 56, 127
  diagnosing epilepsy, 95–96
  spike and wave patterns, 100
Electromyograms, 149
Elks, services for handicapped, 187–188
Emergency services, 211–212
  medical identification, 211–212
Emphysema, 200
Encephalitis, 124
Endodontics, 80
Enzyme disturbances
  muscular dystrophy, 149
  serum enzyme tests, 150
  substitution therapy, 65
  Tay-Sachs disease, 169–170
Epilepsy, 93–101
  aura, 100
  community health information, 97
  description of, 93–94
  drug therapy, 94–96
    anticonvulsant drugs, 94–96
  educational programs, 98–100
  grand mal seizures, 93
  petit mal seizures, 93–95
  recreational programs, 100
  seizures, 93–95, 100–101
  services for, 96–100
  tests, 94, 96
  treatment, 94–95
Epilepsy Association of America, 98
Epilepsy Foundation of America, 97–99
Epileptologists, 97
Erythrocytes, 62
Ethanbutol, 172
Eye diseases, 4
  (See also Blindness)

Factor VIII, 115
Family Service Association of America, 133

Federal aid, 198–199
  mental health services, 138
  (See also National Institutes of Health)
Federal research programs
  allergies and asthma, 10
  arthritis, 17–18
  cancer, 45
  cerebral palsy, 56
  cystic fibrosis, 66–67
  deafness and partial hearing, 72
  dental problems, 80
  diabetes, 86
  drug addiction, 91
  epilepsy, 97
  heart disease, 107
  hemophilia, 114
  kidney disease, 121
  muscular dystrophy, 151
  retardation, 162
  tuberculosis, 174
  venereal disease, 178–179
  (See also National Institutes of Health)
Federation of Jewish Philanthropies, 184
Federation of Protestant Welfare Agencies, 184
Fetology, 22
Flexion, 58
Fluoridation of water, 79, 82
Folic acid, 62, 166
Foot deformities, 21, 24, 155
Forecast (magazine), 87
Foundation for Research and Education in Sickle Cell Disease, 167
Franconi, Dr. Guido, 63
Fraternal organizations, services for the handicapped, 187–188

Gastroenterologists, 66
Genes and chromosomes, 28
Genetic counseling, 22, 27–28
Genetic disorders
  cystic fibrosis, 63
  hemophilia, 111
  muscular dystrophy, 147–154
  National Institute of General Medical Sciences, 204
  sickle-cell anemia, 165–168
  Tay-Sachs disease, 169–171
Geneticists, 60, 151, 170
Genito-urinary malformations, 21
German measles (rubella), 159, 164
  immunization against, 21–22, 27, 55
  rubella vaccine for, 21–22, 53, 70
Gingiva and gingivitis, 78, 82
Girl Scouts, programs for handicapped, 58, 138, 209

Glomerulonephritis, 117
  acute, 119-120, 123
  chronic, 117-118, 123
  treatment, 118-119
Glucose, 83, 84
  blood glucose test, 85
Gonococcus, 180
Gonorrhea, 177-179
Gout, 14
Government services, 198-206
  library services, 205-206
  National Institutes of Health, 198-205
  tax deductions, 206
    (*See also* National Institutes of
      Health)
Granulocytes, 52
Group Health Association of America,
  207-208

Hand-foot syndrome, 168
Hard-of-hearing (*see* Deafness)
Hay fever, 4-6
Health, Education and Welfare,
    Department of
  National Institutes of Health, 198
  Social Rehabilitation Services
    Administration, 162
Health Insurance Institute, 208
Health Insurance Plan of Greater New
    York, 207
Health plans, 207-208
  consumer-sponsored, 207
  insurance information, 208
Hearing difficulties (*see* Deafness)
Hearing and Speech News, 76
Heart disease, 102-110
  American Heart Association, 108-110
  community health information, 106-
    107
  congenital anomalies, 102-103
  description, 102-103
  drug therapy, 103-105
  educational programs, 109-110
  open heart surgery, 103-104, 110
  rheumatic fever and, 102-106, 109
  services available, 106-107
  tests, 105-106
  treatment, 103-105
Hematologists, 44, 50, 60, 114
Hemianopsia, 40
Hemiplegia, 58
Hemoglobin, 60, 62, 165, 168
Hemophilia, 111-116
  clotting factor concentrates, 111-112
  community health information, 114
  description of, 111
  services, 114-115
  treatment, 112

Hemorrhages, 111-112
Henry, Robert, 114
Hereditary disorders
  cystic fibrosis, 63
  muscular dystrophy, 147
  sickle-cell anemia, 165
  Tay-Sachs disease, 170
Heroin addiction, 89
Hexosaminidase component A, 169-171
Histamine, 3, 5, 13
Hitchings, Dr. George, 49
Hodgkin, Dr. Dorothy C., 85
Homemaker-home health aides, 185
Hydrocephalus, 163
Hyperactivity, 126, 161
Hyperacusia, 171
Hyperglycemia, 87
Hyperkinetic condition, 129
Hypertension, 69
Hyperthyroidism, 22
Hypoglycemia, 87, 136

Identification, medical, 211-212
Immunization, 4-5, 64
Immunology, 10
Infectious diseases, 4, 70, 201-202
  strep infections, 103-106, 117-118, 120
Institute for Muscle Disease, 148, 152
Insulin, 84-85, 88
Internists, 86, 174
Iridocyclitis or iritis, 14
Isoniazid, 172

James, William, 133
Joint diseases, 4, 14-15

Keller, Helen, 37
Kernicterus, 163
Ketoacidosis, 83, 88
Kidney disease, 4, 117-123
  acute kidney failure, 119
  acute nephritis, 117
  description of, 117-118
  services, 121-122
  transplantation of kidney, 119
    Organ Donor Program, 122
  treatment, 118-119
    artificial kidney machines, 119, 122
    peritoneal dialysis, 119
    steroids, 118-119
Kidney Foundation, 119
Koch, Robert, 172

Latimer, H. Randolph, 37
Lead poisoning, 159

Learning disabilities, 27, 124-129
  description of, 124-126
  educational program, 126-127
  minimal brain dysfunction, 124-129
  services, 126-128
Leukemia, 44, 48-52
  acute and chronic, 42, 48
  description of, 48
  drug therapy, 49-50
  services available, 50-52
  treatment, 48-49
Leukemia Society of America, 44, 50-52
Leukocytes, 52
Lewis, F. Park, 39
Library of Congress, services for the
  blind and handicapped, 33, 40,
  205-206
Lions International, services for the
  handicapped, 188
Liver, functions of, 62
Local departments of health, 183
Lung-damaging diseases, 67-68, 200-201
  cystic fibrosis, 63
  tuberculosis, 22, 172-176
Lymphocytes, 52
Lymphomas, 52

Macy, Anne Sullivan, 39
Malnutrition, 159
March of Dimes Birth Defect Centers,
  24, 26
Marijuana, 91
Measles (see German measles)
Medic Alert Foundation, 211
Medical identification, 211-212
Medical schools, services for the
  handicapped, 187
Meningitis, 124, 159
Mental Health Associations, 91, 132-
  134
Mental Health Committee, 133
Mental health services, 138-146
  list of state mental authorities and
    state associations, 139-146
Mental illness, 130-146
  autism, 135-139
  community health information,
    132-133
  description, 130-131
    neuroses, 130
    psychoses, 130
  drug therapy, 131-132
  educational programs, 134
  list of state mental health authorities
    and state associations, 139-146
  services available, 132-134
Mental retardation (see Retardation)

Metabolic disorders, 25, 67, 114, 201
  diabetes, 83-88
  inborn errors of metabolic processes,
    24, 29, 86, 147, 159
Metastasis, 48
Methadone, 90
Microcephalus, 164
Milhorat, Dr. Ade T., 152
Mongolism (Down's syndrome), 28
Morphine, 89
"Multiply handicapped" children, 32, 70
Muscles, 154
  hypotonia, 171
  relaxants, 56
Muscular dystrophy, 21, 27, 140-154
  community health information, 151
  description of, 147
  drug therapy, 149
  educational programs, 154
  pseudohypertrophic (Duchenne) type,
    147, 150
  recreational program, 154
  services available, 151-153
  treatment and tests, 147-150
Muscular Dystrophy Association of
  America, 148, 150-152

Narcotics, 89, 91
  (See also Drug addiction)
National Advisory Committee on
  Handicapped Children, 126
National Association for Mental
  Health, 132-134, 146
National Association for Retarded
  Children, 161-164
National Association of Hearing and
  Speech Agencies, 75-76, 186
National Association of Parents and
  Friends of Mentally Retarded
  Children, 162
National Association of the Deaf, 73-74
National Cancer Institute, 45, 50-51,
  107, 199
National Children's Rehabilitation
  Center, 98-99
National Clearinghouse for Drug Abuse
  Information, 91
National Council for Homemaker-Home
  Health Aide Services, 185
National Cystic Fibrosis Research
  Foundation, 66-69
National Easter Seal Society for
  Crippled Children and Adults,
  17, 27, 72, 210
National Education Association, Council
  for Exceptional Children, 196
National Eye Institute, 37, 199-200

National Foundation-March of Dimes, 21-22, 25-27, 155
National Foundation for Infantile Paralysis, 25
National Genetics Foundation, 27-28
National Heart and Lung Institute, 107, 200-201
National Heart Institute, 107
National Hemophilia Foundation, 112, 114-115
National Institute of Allergy and Infectious Diseases, 11, 174, 178-179, 201-202
National Institute of Arthritis and Metabolic Diseases, 17-18, 67, 86, 114, 121, 201
National Institute of Child Health and Human Development, 57, 202
National Institute of Dental Research, 80-81, 202-203
National Institute of Environmental Health Sciences, 203
National Institute of General Medical Sciences, 204
National Institute of Mental Health, 138, 204-205
National Institute of Neurological Diseases and Stroke, 57, 72, 97, 151, 162, 199, 203
National Institutes of Health, 17, 25, 45, 198-205
National Kidney Foundation, 119, 121-122
National Library of Medicine, 198, 204
National Mental Health Foundation, 133-134
National Nephrosis Foundation, 121
National Society for Autistic Children, 133, 136-138, 210
National Society for Crippled Children and Adults, 155
National Society for the Prevention of Blindness, 30, 38-40
National Tay-Sachs and Allied Diseases Association, 170-171
National Tuberculosis and Respiratory Disease Association, 174-175
Nebulizers, 65
Neoplasms, 52
Nephritis, chronic, 120
Nephrologists, 121
Nephrons, 123
Nephrosis, 118-120
  steroid treatment, 118-120
Neprotic syndrome, 123
  blood tests, 120
Neuroblastomas, 42
Neurological disorders, 4, 27, 72, 93-101

Neurologists, 54, 56, 97, 128, 132, 151, 170
Nucleic acids, 149
Nutritionists, 191

Occupational therapists, 17, 54, 56, 128, 191
Ophthalmologists, 32, 128
Opium addiction, 89
Opticians, 33
Optometrists, 32-33, 128
Orthodontia, 78-79, 80
Orthopedic disorders, 27, 155
Orthopedic surgery, 17, 54, 187
Orthopedists, 54, 56, 187, 191
Osteoarthritis, 14
Otto, John C., 111

Pancreas, 83-84
  enzymes, 63-64, 69
Para-aminosalicylic acid (PAS), 172
Paranoia, 135
Paraplegia, 58
Partial hearing, 70-77
  (See also Deafness)
Partial sightedness, 30-32
  (See also Blindness)
Pathologists, 44, 114
Pediatricians, 44, 54, 56, 60, 66, 86, 121, 128, 136, 170, 191
Pedodontics, 80
Penicillin therapy, 4, 177-178
Perceptual handicaps, 124-126, 129
Periodontal diseases, 78-79
Periodontitis, 78, 82
Peritoneal dialysis, 119
Phelps, Winthrop M., 53
Phenylketonuria, 25, 29
Physiatrists (rehabilitation specialists), 151, 187
Physical therapists, 17, 54, 56, 66, 128, 186-187, 191
Pneumonia, 63
Poison emergencies, 211
Polio, 5, 25
Premature births, 53, 55
Prenatal care, 21, 159-160
  amniocentesis, 22, 24, 170
  prevention of retardation, 21, 159-160
Prescription emergency services, 211
President's Committee on Mental Retardation, 160
Prosthetists, 191
Psychiatric Foundation, 134
Psychiatrists, 54, 56, 90, 97, 128, 132, 136
Psychoanalysts, 132
Psychological disorders, 27

Psychologists, 56, 91, 97, 132
Psychotherapy, 32, 135
Public Health Service, 17, 204
Publications and films
  autism, 137–138
  Cooley's anemia, 62
  cystic fibrosis, 68–69
  dental problems, 81
  diabetes, 87
  epilepsy, 99
  hard-of-hearing, 73–76
  heart disease, 109
  hemophilia, 115
  kidney disease, 122
  mental illness, 134
  muscular dystrophy, 153–154
  retardation, 163
  venereal disease, 179
Pulmonary physiologists, 66
Pyelonephritis, 117
Pyorrhea, dental problem, 78

Quadriplegia, 58

Radiation therapy, 43, 48, 49
Recreation for the handicapped, 209–210
  arthritis patients, 19
  cerebral palsy patients, 58
  epilepsy patients, 100
  heart disease patients, 108
  learning disabilities, 129
  muscular dystrophy patients, 154
  summer camps, 87, 138, 209–210
Rehabilitation services
  blind and partially sighted, 31–33
  brain-damaged children, 127
  epilepsy, 98
  hard-of-hearing, 71
  state agencies, 196–197
  vocational counseling, 196–197
Religion-affiliated services, 163,
  184–185
Retardation, 156–164
  community health information, 161
  description, 156–159
  drug therapy, 160–161
  educational programs, 156–160
    preschool programs, 156–158
    training programs, 157–160
  prevention of, 159–160
    prenatal care, 21, 159–160
  services available, 161–163
Retina, 41
Retrolental fibroplasia, 31, 200
Rh-factor incompatability, 22, 55, 70,
  124, 159
  anti-Rh serum, 23, 27

Rheumatic diseases, 14–20, 67
  (See also Arthritis)
Rheumatic fever and heart disease, 14,
  102–106, 109
Rheumatologists, 17–18
Rifampin, 172
Rimland, Dr. Bernard, 137
RNA (ribonucleic acid), 149
Roentgenologists, 66
Roosevelt, Franklin D., 25
Rotary Clubs, services for the
  handicapped, 210
Rubella vaccine, 21–22, 27
  (See also German measles)

Sachs, Dr. Bernard, 169
Salk vaccine, 25
Schizophrenia, 130–131, 135
Schuyler, Louis Lee, 39
Scolosis, 155
Seizures, 100–101, 171
Sickle-cell anemia, 21, 165–168
  community health information, 167
  description of, 165
  screening tests, 166–167
  services, 167
  treatment, 165–166
Silver nitrate for eyes of newborns,
  30, 39, 177
Snellen charts, 40
Social Planning Council, 184
Social workers, 54, 191
Speech disorders, 21, 27
Speech education for deaf children, 71
Speech pathologists, 191
Speech therapists, 54, 56, 128, 136, 186
Speechreading, 71, 75
Spinal taps, 55
Spine, curvature of, 25
State Mental Health Authority, 132–133
State services, 189–197
  Crippled Childrens Programs, 189–
    190
  allergies, 10
  arthritis, 17
  birth defects, 24–25
  cerebral palsy, 56
  clinics, 190–191
  cystic fibrosis, 66–67
  epilepsy, 97
  heart disease, 107
  muscular dystrophy, 151
  orthopedic and physically handi-
    capping conditions, 155
  retardation, 161–162
  description of, 189–191
  eligibility requirements, 190–192
  list of state agencies, 139–146, 192–196

State services *(cont.)*:
  mental health services, 138–139
    facilities, 138–139
    federal aid, 138
    list of state mental authorities and
      state associations, 139–146
  special education programs, 196–197
Steroid treatment, 118–119
Streptococcus infections, 117–118, 120
  heart disease and, 103–106
Surgery, 80, 191
  birth defects, 23
  open-heart, 103–104, 110
  orthopedic, 17, 54, 187
Synanon, drug treatment centers, 91
Synovectomy and synovial membrane,
  17, 20
Syphilis, 177–179
  acute and chronic, 177
  congenital, 177, 179
  treatment, 178–179
  (*See also* Venereal disease)

Tax deductions, 206
Tay, Warren, 169
Tay-Sachs disease, 169–171, 203
  description, 169
  treatment, 169–170
Tests and testing
  allergies, 7
  brain-damaged children, 127–128
  cerebral palsy, 55–56
  cystic fibrosis, 65–66
  diabetes, 85
  hearing loss, 70–71
  heart disease, 105–106
  hemophilia, 113
  intelligence tests, 128
  kidney disease, 120
  muscular dystrophy, 149–150
  retardation, 161
  sickle-cell anemia, 166–167
  Tay-Sachs disease, 170
  tuberculosis, 173
  venereal disease, 180
Tetanus, immunization, 5
Thalassanemia major and minor, 59
Tooth decay (*see* Dental problems)
Toxoplasmosis, 159
Tranquilizers, 56, 131–132, 160–161

Transplantation, 119, 121–122
  heart, 103–104
  kidney, 119, 121–122
Tuberculosis, 22, 172–176
  allergic reactions and, 4
  community health information, 174
  description of, 172
  services, 174–176
  treatment, 172–173
Tumors, 42–43, 47–48, 52, 55

United Cerebral Palsy Association,
  56–58
United Community Funds and Councils
  of America, 184
United Funds, 184
United States Public Health Service,
  17, 204
Universities, services for the
  handicapped, 187
Urea, 166
Urinary tract obstructive diseases, 118
Urine, 120
  output of creatinine, 150, 154
  tests, 120

Venereal disease, 22, 177–180
  community health information, 178
  description of, 177
  services, 178–179
  treatment, 177–178
Visiting Nurse Association, 185–186
Visiting nurse services, 184–186
Vitamin therapy, 65, 136, 166
Vocational rehabilitation, 98, 127,
  196–197
Volta Bureau, 74
Volta Review, The, 75

Washington Sounds (newsletter), 76
Webbed fingers or toes, 155
Whooping cough, immunization, 5
Wilms' tumor, 42
World Health Organization, 92
World Medical Assembly, 212

X-rays, 66, 79